A Chrysler Chronicle

A
Chrysler
CHRONICLE

One Man's Story of Restoring
a Classic 1948 New Yorker

—— DAVE FLOYD ——

McFarland & Company, Inc., Publishers
Jefferson, North Carolina, and London

Library of Congress Cataloguing-in-Publication Data

Floyd, Dave, 1953–
    A Chrysler chronicle : one man's story of restoring a classic
1948 New Yorker / Dave Floyd.
        p.   cm.
    Includes index.
    ISBN 0-7864-0910-X (softcover : 60# alkaline paper) ∞
    1. Chrysler automobile—Conservation and restoration.
2. Floyd, Dave, 1953–   3. Mechanics (Persons)—United States.
I. Title.
TL215.C55F58   2000
629.28'722—dc21   00-58382

British Library cataloguing data are available

Manufactured in the United States of America

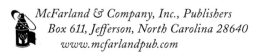
*McFarland & Company, Inc., Publishers
    Box 611, Jefferson, North Carolina 28640
        www.mcfarlandpub.com*

To my lovely wife Ginny,
my daughters Sarah and Emily,
my unborn grandchildren, Robert Floyd, Brandon Krick and
all the vehicles of the world that are beckoning for restoration.

In Loving Memory

Edwin Floyd

Gertrude Moore

Jeanette Silbaugh

William Gross

Carl Moore

Wesley Hughes

Fred Ducane

Clint Johnson

William Peedan

Acknowledgments

I am grateful to the following for materials and information provided: Daimler Chrysler and Crank and Hope Publishing for excerpts from the *1948 Chrysler Shop Manual*; Hearst Business Media, for material from *Motor's Auto Repair Manual 1951*; and Krause Publications, for material from the *Standard Catalog of American Cars*.

Contents

Introduction

My interest in automobiles began as a child in Port Hueneme, California, when I used to ride around town in the back seat of my Dad's 1958 Ford nine-passenger station wagon. I would amaze my two sisters by having the knack to not only name the different makes of cars as they went by, but also to tell them the year and model. This ability I suppose came from reading magazines and seeing the car advertisements on television. A lifelong love for cars had begun.

In April of 1963 I was nine years old when my father passed away. My mother's younger brother Bill moved into our house to help with the expenses. My mother was 37 years old and raising five children. My Uncle Bill, who was a bachelor at the time and in his middle thirties, filled the void in my life. We went to the Riverside 500 stock car race for several years in a row. Uncle Bill called it the Dan Gurney 500. I loved to sit in the "esses" near turn six. From there I grew up watching the greatest drivers in the world, men like Richard Petty, Scotty Cain, Parnelli Jones, A.J. Foyt and Joe Weatherly.

We also went to the drag races a lot with my older brother George. What a thrill it was to watch "Dandy" Dick Landy and "Big Daddy" Ed Roth. I remember the day we watched Bursette and Sutherland break the track record at the San Fernando Dragway when they turned 219 mph, after blowing up a motor on the first attempt. Uncle Bill also took me to the big name car shows like Mickey Thompson, at the Shrine Auditorium in downtown Los Angeles.

I continued to enjoy all sorts of motorsports and was always a fan of the drags. When I turned 16 years old and was ready to buy my first car, my sister's boyfriend (and now husband for over 30 years), Dick, helped me seek and find it. It was a 1957 Ford Ranchero—but not the normal variety. It had been modified by a guy who lived out on the Strand and was powered by a 383 cubic inch Mercury police interceptor V-8. Dick and I were always in the garage wrenching on something. My favorite was a 1958 English Ford Anglia purchased jointly by Dick and George. For an engine the firewall was cut out and a Ford V-8 Flathead was put in. The rear seat had to be taken out to make room for the driver's seat. Dick Brown probably had the most influence in the development of my mechanical ability. We rebuilt several engines together and Dick made many sacrifices teaching me most of what I know about auto mechanics today.

I joined the U.S. Army in 1975. My military occupational skill was that of helicopter repairman; I went to school at the Army Aviation Center, Fort Rucker, Alabama. It was a fantastic experience and one that introduced me to my wife Ginny. I was stationed in Ansbach, West Germany, when my roommate Robert Neff's sister came to visit him. We were introduced and hit it off—this year we will celebrate our twentieth wedding anniversary.

Upon completion of my tour of duty, Ginny convinced me to carry on with my education so I attended the airframe and powerplant mechanics course at the West Los Angeles Airport College Center. Ginny and I were blessed with our first daughter, Sarah, in 1980 while I was going to school and she worked as a dental assistant in Marina Del Rey. During my last semester of school I submitted an application to the National Aeronautics and Space Administration when a representative visited the campus in effort to recruit aircraft maintenance technicians. I was accepted in the winter of 1980 as a co-op student and was offered a full time position in June of the following year.

We packed up all of our belongings in Inglewood, California, and the three of us headed off to begin a new life. Our second daughter, Emily, was born in 1982. I continued my education taking full advantage of the benefits offered with the Veterans Administration, achieving an associate of arts and an associate science degree from the Antelope Valley Community College.

During my tenure at NASA I have been trained and certified in five different methods of non-destructive testing and have completed several courses in the field of advanced composites and quality assurance. I have worked on a variety of experimental aircraft such as the Support B-52, HIMAT (highly maneuverable aircraft technology), F-15 Spin Research Vehicle, X-29 Forward Swept Wing, F/A-18 High Angle of Attack Research Vehicle, F-104, F-111 Ejection Capsule Test Article, Space Shuttle Rocket Booster Parachute Test Article, X-31 Enhanced Fighter Maneuverability, X-38 Crew Recovery Vehicle and the SR-71.

For a long time my friends at work tried to encourage me to buy a motorcycle so we could all go for rides together on weekends and holidays. I love motorcycles and have had three or four in my life. This was a good thought and I admire my friends for who they are and what they do, but practical considerations would weigh differently. My wife and two daughters couldn't fit on the back of one bike, and Ginny was neither experienced nor willing to ride her own bike, much less with Sarah or Emily on the back. At any rate, the cost of two road bikes was a bit more than our family could afford.

We always have done things together as a family. We camped together, we took family vacations, we did the Girl Scout thing, we visited factories and museums. We had all worked together putting up a swimming pool in the back yard; the girls and I even built a room addition to our house together.

It occurred to me that if we restored an old car, we could continue to do our thing together more easily. Ginny and I discussed the matter and decided to do it, so we set out on our new goal. We would never regret one minute of the adventure that followed.

I was always on the lookout for a good deal on an old car anywhere at any time, just as a matter of habit, but now that we had decided to restore one I intensified my search. I began looking for old vehicles around town, like the ones you see parked in yards and alleys and storage yards. I read the newspaper, bulletin boards and throw-away papers. This lasted about five months until a special car came along.

1

David Meets Goliath

On February 4, 1991, I answered an ad in the local *Desert Mailer* classified paper for the sale of a 1948 Chrysler New Yorker. The ad was listed in the Antique and Classic section. Upon arriving at Mr. George Judson's house in Lancaster, I met the owner, Mr. Bill Zamboni, and looked the car over.

Anyone in a similar position should take a photo of the vehicle *now*, as you first see it. Photograph it exactly how and where it sits and from several angles. This is what I did not do, but my recollection is as follows.

The hood was opened about halfway; the air cleaner was off resting in another area of the engine compartment. The wiring looked old and some of the insulation had weathered away. The engine compartment as a whole was coated with a ⅛-inch layer of good ol' desert blow sand. A sand dune had started to form on the left side of the car, almost reaching the lower doorsill. All four of the whitewall tires were flat; the roof had a large dent (which I found out later was inflicted by a fallen tree limb during a spring breeze of about 50 mph). All fenders had experienced the rigors of the road and endless encounters in the parking lots and within the garage. There were dents on every corner of the car, but it was all there.

In the back seat, opening the door for the first time, I took in the unmistakable odor of musty wet wool. I noted also that the left rear interior door panel had a hole punched into it. Evidently this happened when the axle lying on the rear floor protruded as the door was slammed shut. One must be able to see past the layers of dust, grease and sand.

After lengthy discussion and observation of the vehicle Mr. Zamboni agreed to a selling price of $650. In the course of our transaction I learned that Mr. Zamboni had purchased the car from Saul and Gertrude Montrose of Palmdale, California, in August of 1990—just six months earlier—and transported it to Mr. Judson's house for storage. Mr. Zamboni had made the acquaintance of Mr. and Mrs. Montose's daughter Melinda, which in turn led him to make the purchase. At the time he had plans and high hopes of conducting his own restoration.

In further discussion I learned that while the car was being towed from Palmdale to Lancaster the rear end had locked up and Mr. Zamboni had had to complete his journey via tow truck to the spot where the car rested now, when I purchased it. Mr. Zamboni had not done any work at all on the vehicle while it was in his possession.

Also, I learned that Mr. Montrose was holding the original engine at his home. The motor had been changed in 1972 because of a seized piston, but the car had not been registered since 1972. It had been sitting in the Montrose driveway for 18 years, sometimes covered and protected and sometimes not.

I found out later in a visit with Mrs. Montrose that she would sometimes spend her time outside washing and waxing the old family car. It was her love, dedication and memories that moved her to perform this act; after all it had been the family car since 1958. They purchased it used from Redman Chrysler-Plymouth in Lancaster. It was also during this time in the driveway that the tree limb I mentioned earlier had crashed upon the car roof.

The car as I purchased it was complete with all parts, chrome, glass, etc. It was rough looking, in fair but weathered condition. I knew in my heart that some elbow grease and tender loving care would

Left: **In this booklet I found much about the vehicle's history.** *Right:* **Notice the telephone number—this is before area codes.**

produce gainful results. Added to the deal were a new wiring harness (still in the box), a used but good radiator, an original 1951 printing of a *Motor's Auto Repair Manual* and even the engine at Saul's house.

I plan someday to rebuild this old motor and reunite the original equipment. To collectors this is known as matching numbers and is considered an extremely important added value.

In the glove compartment, untouched since 1972, were numerous receipts, a repair record and many other small items such as clothespins, matches, and a quick reference guide on what to do in the event of nuclear attack. Opening the glove compartment and searching its contents was like opening a time capsule. There were gasoline receipts for 32.9 cents a gallon; a fill-up was $4.62. Attached

17

Found in the glovebox.

to a set of spare keys I found a miniature license plate, purchased from the Disabled American Veterans, that would guarantee the postage and return of the lost or found keys to the owner. I remember my own parents having such a plate back in the 1960s. But wait, the number on this miniplate actually matched the one on the car! Each little discovery increased my excitement.

The repair record book showed an oil change on June 21 at

99,550 miles. The mileage odometer on the car read 101,430; the oil was changed 1880 miles back. Even though I realized it might not have been on this motor, I knew that persons who kept such records were concerned enough to take proper care of things. The generator and regulator were overhauled at 98,861 miles; the muffler was replaced at 96,656 for a cost of $24.70. The first entry of the record book was made on February 3, 1964 (almost 27 years ago to the day), for 18.7 gallons of gasoline, costing $6.35.

Completing the transaction with Mr. Zamboni, I received the pink slip and registration, still in the name of Saul and Gertrude Montrose. I arranged with Mr. Judson to return the following Saturday and remove the car.

Just like that, I had the car. Not because it was a Chrysler or anything else for that matter, but because it was a dream I had wanted to fulfill for quite some time. I had always wanted to get a car, any car, from the 1940s and restore it. The cars back then were made to last and the engineering that made them was of an enduring technology which helped our country achieve a position of world leadership. The price was right, and the car was in just the right condition, complete and showing no rust at all. When a car spends its entire life in the excellent high desert environment of California, it will be a well preserved specimen when it comes to corrosion. The undercoating on the car was as good as when it came off of the assembly line, with the exception of age.

It all takes off from here. The next day I visited my credit union and found a book with prices, production numbers, specifications and a brief history of the car. Although the book I referred to was already ten years old, I discovered that all my old swap meet and garage sale bargaining practices had paid off. My estimations of the car and its condition on a rating scale of 1 through 5 by the book calculated a value of $1800, and this book was ten years old. "Gold mine city," I thought to myself. Why, just that trip through the glove compartment was worth $300 to me. The damage to the car described earlier was not a factor in my calculations since restoration included repair in the process.

I learned a few more facts that day in the book too. The serial numbers listed in 1948 for the Chrysler New Yorker Sedan were from 7,062,598 to 7,085,469. My serial number was 7,078,683. Math time! I had the 16,085th car off the line of a 22,871-car production in 1948. What day of the week was that? What month could it have been? I bet a lot of World War II veterans home after the war and raising families earned a paycheck building my new old car. I sat there staring at the picture of a shiny Chrysler New Yorker. It was just like mine would be soon. It had a luggage rack on top, mine didn't, but that was okay. Mine had options that weren't in this picture, like a windshield mounted sun and snow visor, two big chrome plated push bars and two very large amber colored fog lamps. I knew that they weren't aftermarket pieces because right there on top was the MOPAR stamp.

Suddenly, it began to occur to me that finally, just maybe, things were starting to go my way. If ever a man would have it all, it would be me. My occupation as an aircraft mechanic (actually Aerospace Engineering Technician, GS 802) for NASA had always been good to me and being assigned on the most recent of the famous X-Planes, the X-29 Forward Swept Wing Aircraft, had surely had it moments. What a privilege, I often thought. And now I had the chance to bring this sturdy old Chrysler back to its full glory.

After the credit union visit I returned to the hangar where I ran into a good friend, Artie Hartington. Artie, also assigned to the X-29, was working with Grumman Aircraft, who built the bird. I wasn't thinking of it at the time when I told Artie about my most recent purchase, but he too is a follower of antique cars and stayed pretty much up to date with the current markets and information. I no sooner got parts of the story out of my mouth about the Chrysler than Artie thrust a fairly recent copy of *Hemmings Motor News* into my hand. He said simply, "You'll be needing this."

As the news about my car was traded around the breakroom at lunch, I noticed the "sparkle" in the eyes of all the, shall we say, "older guys." When we talked about my car, they shared stories of their own old cars or those of their parents, uncles and grandparents. Just the mention of an old car and ears popped up and eyes gleamed.

I had never realized the mutual regard for cars and the role they played in people's lives till now. I was in the beginning stages of an association, a fraternity, erudition.

Up to now I haven't mentioned much about my family, but they were the reason for purchasing the car and they were with me when I bought it. We needed something we could all do together. My wife Ginny, who has always been supportive of me, didn't hesitate at all when I asked if she thought we could afford $650 to buy the car. Quite frankly, we didn't have the money at the time, but when you see a deal like this, well, it's just time to dip into the overdraft. Our income taxes were just mailed in and we would repay the overdraft when the tax return came. A very important development to my story soon came about when Sarah and Emily announced, "Let's name it Goliath!" Why? Well, my name is David, and when the girls realized what a giant undertaking this would be, another piece fell into place. Children can be rather imaginative sometimes in their reasoning. They must have conjured this up earlier, but we all agreed "Goliath" it was. The fact that my girls came up with the name may account for some of my enthusiasm for it, but there are no rules here, even though most nicknames for cars I have encountered do favor the female gender.

The magic of the old car was soon to blossom for another individual. It was the following Saturday now, the day I had told Mr. Judson that I would come for the car. That morning I phoned around looking for a tow truck service that could move Goliath for a good price. Tumbleweed Towing agreed to do the job for $30. I went to Mr. Judson's house and prepared the car by adding air to all the tires, changing out one with the spare tire because it would not hold air, and securing the hood. But when the appointed time came, the driver from Tumbleweed was held up at another job and wouldn't be able to come until Sunday. My sharp disappointment must have come out, and the driver gave me the number of another tow truck operator by the name of Pat. He too owned a tow truck hiring out for small jobs like mine on the weekends for the same price.

Pat was on the scene with his younger son less than 45 minutes after my call. I met him out front and directed him to the rear of Mr. Judson's house. As we rounded a corner and Goliath came into view, I noticed the expression on his face change. He said something in Spanish, then proceeded to explain how he could connect me with all sorts of people who did upholstery, body work (lead fill if I wanted) and mechanical work on vintage vehicles. We secured the car, very carefully, with intense concentration and instruction to his son. Pat showed the boy how to do this type of lift.

We drove westbound towards my house with Pat and his son following. I couldn't help looking in the rear view mirror as we traveled and I could see Pat talking to his son as he slowed down for every bump in the road. At cross streets he carefully navigated the dips and chuckholes to avoid any undue or extraneous load on the car. His son was getting an earful, I'm sure.

We arrived at my house unscathed and fully intact. It was a typical February day and starting to rain lightly, but that didn't stop the neighbors from coming out to see what was going on. First it was Dennis across the street, then Johnny next door. As Pat backed Goliath up the driveway and maneuvered into the position I had designated, something beautiful happened. I stood there in the driveway feeling as if I had been shot forward in time. The rain had coated Goliath now, and through the magic of water glistening, I could see the original color appear instantly as the rain absorbed all those years of oxidation just like that. The original dark blue, I decided, would remain the paint color.

2

Down to Business

Two months and $300 later, Goliath sat in the same corner spot of the driveway, elevated by four jack stands with the rear end and all wheel and brake assemblies removed. It had been vacuumed thoroughly inside and just for fun I added a coat of wax to see how much color would come out with some oxidation removed.

The differential, which had seized during the towing of the New Yorker from Palmdale eight months earlier as I mentioned earlier, had probably occurred because while the vehicle was sitting at the Montrose home for all of those 18 years, the gear oil leaked, seeped or congealed to zero. We all know what happens to moving metal parts that require lubrication when they have none. I suspected the pinion bearing had heated to such a degree that one, two or several ball bearings had come out of their housing, moved freely as foreign objects inside the third member casings and then become lodged in the meshing differential gears resulting in lockup, sudden stoppage. A wrench in the cogs, so to speak.

Lesson to be learned: If you decide to tow a vehicle that has been parked for some time, service all fluid levels before attempting to travel.

I wanted to pick up the car's original engine as soon as possible lest it be discarded. I phoned my good friend and coworker Dan Bain, on whom I could always depend in time of need, even on short notice.

On Sunday morning, February 10, Dan and I took my 1971 Chevy pickup to the Montrose residence in Palmdale, enjoying the beautiful view of the San Gabriel Mountains from the Sierra Highway. The day was crisp and clear and we could see well over 50 miles.

When we arrived at the Montrose residence I met Saul for the first time, finding him younger than I had imagined when speaking to him by phone.

He was pleased that someone was going to undertake the restoration of what had been the family car for many years. Saul led Dan and me through a side gate of the house and there on the back patio sat an enormous mass of iron four feet long and three feet high, covered with a blue waterproof tarp and cotton cord. The oil pan, crankshaft, pistons and rods had already been disassembled, and the engine sat flat atop a four wheel dolly. Next to the engine were two boxes filled with miscellaneous parts and accessories. I was trying to inventory this in my head as Saul reminisced about driving the Chrysler on family vacations.

I should have paid more attention to his conversation, but in my mind I was trying to plan how we would get all of this iron into the truck. It was easy enough to wheel the engine out to the front of the house on the dolly, but getting it up into the truckbed was another matter. Dan and I sat scratching our heads. I suggested placing a couple of boards from the ground to the truck as a ramp, but Dan was quick to point out that the weight might cause the boards to break. That would not be a good thing! Dan suggested that we disconnect the tailgate from its two side supports and let it hang down. Thus it provided a ramp of sorts. Standing one on each side we lifted the front wheels of the dolly onto the tailgate. The engine and dolly rested in place at about a 40-degree angle. Dan attached a nylon strap under and around the front wheels. He then hopped into the truck and lifted and pulled as I lifted and pushed from behind. Half a hernia later we were on our way home again. Saul wanted the dolly back but was in no hurry, so we were able to use it in offloading the engine back at home.

The first photo on the second day after Goliath was brought to my house.

When the rear end was removed and disassembled my suspicions were confirmed. The sudden stoppage during the 12-mile tow had created such forces as to literally rip free from their welds the mounting brackets that held the rear end to the leaf springs. Upon complete inspection I determined that the axles were undamaged and that no twisting had occurred during the lockup, likely because the tires had skidded. The gears, however, were badly chipped and broken.

I enlisted the help of my good friend Ed Swan, expert certified welder, to help me clean up, straighten and weld together again the exterior mounting brackets. At the time we did this repair we had no specifications or manuals which stated the exact angle at which we should recouple the brackets by metal fusion process. No one at the local Chrysler dealer knew either. Ed, drawing on his knowledge of metallurgy and extensive experience, decided the proper angles after closely examining the torn metal and taking some measurements of the driveline.

I now sought to find a replacement third member. Several phone calls around to the Antelope Valley area auto dismantlers yielded no results until I phoned Glendale Auto Salvage on 90th Street East in Lancaster. The guy on the phone said he didn't have anything that he knew of right off the top of his head. But he did have a 1951 Chrysler out back and also an old bus full of rear end parts. It was a short 10-mile drive, so I decided to go take a gander. I brought along the old third member just in case, having learned from many past experiences always to bring the part along to match it up.

Lo and behold, after an hour of searching around cars and finally in the old bus, there it was, a perfect specimen. So far so good; the part numbers were identical. A count of the gear teeth confirmed that the part was right. Some negotiating with the guy at the counter and I was outta there for $59 including tax and on my way to tackle another step in favor of progress.

On the way home I decided that after I got the car back on the ground, I would get it started and drive it around some before I pulled the engine and transmission for restoration. The urge to roll down the highway was overwhelming my concerns about the possibility that more costly things might crop up.

The downtime while the engine and transmission were out would be the right time, I thought, to install the new wiring harness, do the body work, paint the car and reupholster the interior. It was all work now, and Goliath's newness around the neighborhood had worn off. "She" had become an accepted part of the scenery.

For the remainder of February and on into March I cleaned parts, did more research and read to learn more about the car. This newfound love kindled my desire to rediscover a lost part of myself that I hadn't felt since the good old days in high school. Cars, mechanical

Here the condition of the paint can be seen, soon after I acquired the car.

The tree limb crunch is visible toward the rear of the roof. Damage on the right rear fender is also shown.

things, moving parts, grease, oil, power, speed and the wonderful odor of 90-W gear oil. I love it. What a lucky man I am.

I determined in this time that in order to do a professional job on the car, I would at minimum have to replace all of the brake wheel cylinders and possibly the shoe linings. Inspection showed that these parts, exposed to the elements for so long (even in the perfect climate of the Mojave desert), had deteriorated. Brakes are no place to cut corners, especially if you intend to carry loved ones or cruise mountain roads.

An underhood view, basically as I first saw the car. The effect is not the same as a photograph taken on first sight, though.

On March 23, 1991, I purchased two more jack stands at Chief Auto Parts for $8.49, tax included. This was a bargain, and a stroke of luck. When I went first to Pep Boys they were sold out of the advertised special. So I drove two blocks down the street to Chief Auto Parts, showed the guy there the Pep Boys advertised price, told him I was restoring a 1948 Chrysler and he sold me their $17 pair for $7.99. (Zing ... magic, I tell you, It must have been.)

March 24, 1991: purchased a ½-inch drive torque wrench for use in upcoming differential overhaul. Cost: $7.50. Also on March 24,

The interior as it looked when I brought the car home. Barely visible in the bottom inward portion of the rear door panel is the hole punched by the axle.

I raised the car and put it up on all four jack stands as I mentioned before. I removed the front wheels, brake drums, brake shoes, wheel cylinders and hydraulic interconnect hoses. "What is well begun is half done," I thought; one step at a time.

I learned from reading the *Motor's Auto Repair Manual* that these were dual cylinder, single piston type, hydraulically actuated brakes on the front of the car, manufactured by Lockheed Company. More than likely, I figured, a spinoff of their aircraft technology. Rather peculiar though, in comparison to the dual actuating two-piston single cylinders found on the rear brakes. The front had two single piston (dead ended) cylinders, one for each shoe, whereas the

A closeup view after everything gained in the deal was removed.

rears used one cylinder with two pistons acting in both directions, applying outward force on two shoes simultaneously. Could this have been a safety minded feature on the front brakes, I thought, in the event of one cylinder failing? The manual didn't cover topics like this, so I noted it for future research.

In between all of the solvent baths, hosing off and wire brushing sessions, I was still price shopping and contemplating what other parts I would need to carry out the restoration. The front wheel bearings and grease seals were carefully removed. A cleaning solvent soak followed by air drying of the bearings was done. The wheel bearings and the races (located within the drums) were inspected for wear, color, corrosion and slop.

The color of the bearing and the races is important to observe as it can tell if the bearing has overheated or run without adequate lubrication. A good bearing and race should have a shiny, very highly polished appearance. It is also necessary to reinstall the same bearing and race together in the same location from which they were removed. The wheel bearings were repacked with high temperature wheel bearing grease, then placed in plastic wrap from the kitchen to protect them from contamination of dirt and dust until needed for installation.

The hand packing method of repacking a wheel bearing is to ensure that adequate lubrication enters the inside part of the cage. This is done by donning rubber or disposable latex gloves. Place a fair amount of wheel bearing grease (2 oz.) in the palm of one hand. Hold the bearing in the other hand in such a manner that the widest part of the cone receives the grease first. Press down firmly into the grease, rotating the whole bearing (not spinning) 360 degrees until you can see grease exit the top of the bearing cone from behind the rollers. Now, slowly turn the bearing by hand two revolutions and repeat the above.

All of the brake drums were cleaned and checked for wear, cracks, and general condition, then were repainted. The rear axle bearings were treated the same as the front except that rather than press off and back onto the shafts, I elected to keep them in place on the axles. My inspection revealed no corrosion where they contacted the axles and to preclude a likelihood of damage while removing and installing them, I was better off to leave well enough alone. I figured to date I had spent $20 on several types of cleaners.

Saturday, March 30, the rear end was completed and ready for assembly. I had put paint on some select gear teeth and hand turned the gears through one revolution to inspect for mesh contact in both forward and reverse. The free/endplay on all moving parts appeared not to be excessive. I was gambling on whatever the salvaged third member was removed from, but it was in okay condition now. I paid

Another inside view on Day 2. The dashboard and window frame would not require painting in the restoration.

Yarman Drive Shafts $15 labor to remove and press in a new pinion seal for the third member so that I could put it together. Removing the drive yoke, or universal knuckle as some mechanics call it, required tools, including a ½-inch impact gun, which I did not own.

All the parts fit into place with no problems and I just sat there admiring the shiny, freshly painted rear end I had just completed. I torqued all of the bolts to specification and just the right amount of red sealant oozed out between the flanges as I made one final round with the torque wrench. This was the first job completed on Goliath.

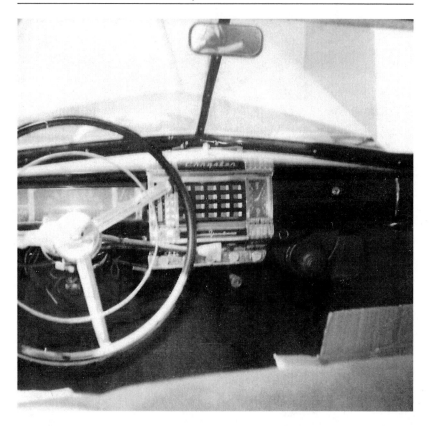

All of the interior chrome needed only a cleaning with 000 steel wool and a good polish.

By the middle of the last week in March I had decided it would be wise to overhaul the rear brakes as well. Kaos Auto Parts on Yucca Ave in Lancaster had beat all other places out in pricing, but what I needed cost more than I could put out at once. I would do a little here, then clean something else, research some, and do a little later. On April 2, 1991, I started ordering my parts. The two rear wheel cylinders were $32 each. I ordered them and got them seven days later for a total of $64 (Safe Line Brake Parts, P/N W10588).

On April 9, 1991, I ordered front wheel cylinders ($17 each × 4 = $68.00). They arrived April 12. On April 15 I ordered brake flex hoses

Top: Early in the restoration, the rear end was removed to begin the task of rewelding the two torn brackets that attached the unit to the vehicle. *Bottom:* The wraparound bumper measured over eight feet from tip to tip. The gasoline tank is located between the two leaf springs aft of the differential and rear end case.

After welding the two torn metal brackets, the third member was installed and torqued into place. A fresh coat of high gloss black paint was applied to finalize the first milestone.

($10.20 each × 3 = $30.60). Why three, you ask? The front wheels with coil spring suspension require individual hoses, while the rear line need only connect in one place and the fluid tubing is rigid (hardline) out to each rear brake. I received the ordered parts April 17.

These parts and many more to come were paid for, by the way, from money Ginny had earned housecleaning and babysitting. She never hesitated at the end of the week when she totaled her earnings if I asked for $60 or $80. Normally we used her money for family outings and entertainment, but lately we did less of that and more work on Goliath.

Pictured here is the driveshaft. Note the universal joint at bottom left. This is the universal that took the brunt of force when the rear end locked up in transit from Palmdale to Lancaster. Notice also that there are no needle bearings or retainer caps that hold them. Likely they scattered in the roadway.

Earlier in this same month I mailed a check to Old Cars in Indianapolis as payment for a new master brake cylinder at a cost of $75 ($50 cheaper than anyone else). After waiting three weeks, I called and the guy from Old Cars said he had never received my check. I stopped payment on the check. It cost me $10 and he sent me the master cylinder cash on delivery (C.O.D.). A very neat way of doing business, but it costs more to do it that way. Some delivery people will even let you inspect the parts first.

The Lockheed dual cylinder, single piston front brake. Pictured here is the left front. Note the excellent condition of all suspension components and the rubber bushings. Because of the TLC given this car by the previous owners it did not need to be disassembled and overhauled for restoration. I needed only to clean, polish and repaint most of the components. The new brake flex hoses are necessary for safety.

On April 25, 1991, I took the front brake shoes to be relined at North Division Brake. Although they appeared to have slightly more than 50 percent wear, my objective was to go all the way. The rear brake shoes on the other hand measured 3/16-inch thickness, which indicated practically new according to the specs in the repair manual.

On April 27 I discovered the first missing part on the car. While cleaning and lubricating in the area of the removed master cylinder I noticed the clutch pedal sort of tilting to one side. The pivot bushing was gone. This is a two piece ball and socket bushing, and hard to replace. That is, of course, unless you can make one. I took the one good half to another good friend of mine, Wes Hughes, and he machined a perfect duplicate. A dozen doughnuts for Wes to stay after hours and do this for me. What are friends for?

The left front shown with reworked shoe linings, brake drum and wheel bearings installed.

Friday May 3, I reassembled the clutch pivot, lubed it and began reinstalling the rear end. The assembly went well, and what a sight to behold! With all parts cleaned up, wire wheeled to original or repainted, and the rewelded brackets in place, it looked just like a new piece taken off the assembly line back in 1948. I was happy and proud of myself.

On May 6 I picked up the brake shoes (cost $38) and the next day I completed the brake support installation on the rear differential housing. This is the round plate piece that bolts to the axle and onto which all of the brake parts and wheel cylinders mount. The brake shoes were installed along with the new wheels cylinders, complete with all associated hardware and springs. The rear brake drums were installed and a brake adjustment was done using an alternate method prescribed by the *Motor's Auto Repair Manual* since I did not have the special tool that is preferred:

ADJUSTMENT WITHOUT GAUGE OR DUMMY
DRUM—If either of these appliances is not available, a
major adjustment of Lockheed brakes may be accomplished as follows:

1. If the eccentric anchor pins are not provided with
   means for turning with a screwdriver or wrench,
   remove them from the support plates, grind off the
   case-hardened surface and slot the end with two hacksaw blades placed side by side in the same frame. Slot
   all anchor pins in a like location. Then mark with a
   prick punch the highest point of the eccentric. This is
   indicated by arrows on some brakes.
2. Replace the anchors and shoes and turn the anchors so
   that the punch marks are together inward, or that the
   points on the arrows are facing each other.
3. Turn the adjusting cams to bring the shoes as far as
   possible away from the drum.
4. Adjust one shoe at a time, turning the cam out until
   the shoe just drags.
5. Turn anchor until drum turns freely. Note that the
   movement of the anchor lowers the shoe so that the
   toe of the shoe no longer drags.
6. Again turn the eccentric cam until toe of shoe just
   drags on drum.
7. Then turn anchor in same direction until drum turns
   freely.
8. Repeat the above until further turning of anchor will
   not free the drum from the drag obtained by setting
   the cam.
9. Then back off both anchor and cam very slightly until
   drum turns freely.
10. Repeat the above procedure on all shoes, and brake
    adjustment very close to the tolerance of .005" clearance at the heel and .010" at the toe will be obtained.

The axle shaft endplay check yielded a perfect .005", a superb
shim job considering that the tolerance called out in the manual was
.003 to .008. The stacking of different thickness shims is required here
as it is on several axles, to provide the proper amount of play necessary so as not to be too tight or too loose. Some measured tolerance

The single cylinder, dual piston Lockheed brake, pictured here on the left rear connected to the reworked rear end.

is required to allow heat expansion of the parts. Because of their superior condition I used the same metal shims from the old assembly, not knowing if the new added third member would have an effect.

To accomplish the endplay measurement I borrowed a dial gauge from Johnny next door and taped it onto a flexible desk lamp held firmly to the ground with a cloth bag full of sand. In and out I repeated the axle movement and it consistently read the same results. Improvise as needed! It was satisfactory to suit my needs.

On May 8 I received a reprint copy of the original shop manual on Chryslers 1941 to 1948 (Dragich Discount Auto Literature catalog #1301, cost $24.95 plus tax and postage, total $29, from an ad in Hemmings Motor News). What a help. I still had more reading and research to do but it was easier now. This book was far more detailed than what I had before, being solely dedicated to my vehicle, Chrysler C-39 (official talk now).

The left rear drum installed. A retainer nut and a tapered key affair hold this drum in place. Most often a drum puller is needed to remove the drum. The lug screws that attach the wheels to the installed drum are reverse thread on the left side of the vehicle.

Friday, May 10, 1991, I assembled the left and right front brake supports. This entails assembly of the brake shoes, wheel cylinders and brake lines connecting the upper and lower cylinders, anchor bolts and return springs. I managed to find exact replacement springs at Jason's Auto Parts in Palmdale ($5.50 each × 4 = $22).

On Saturday morning, May 11, I finished writing up an account of what I had done so far. It did not occur to me until about two months earlier that I should make a record of all this history, and up to now I used scrap paper and index cards to manage my notes. Now I began a more systematic effort, keeping a diary that would eventually form the basis for this book.

The next day, Sunday May 12, I found that with the front brake assemblies and brake supports installed onto the axles, there was no way that the brake drums would fit over the shoes without damaging the new linings; the circumference was too large. One step forward and two steps back today.

Tuesday, May 14, I removed the entire brake assembly on the left side of the car and just the drum and shoes on the right. This was so I could return to North Division Brake and analyze the drum fit. By the time I had them all removed it was too late in the day to visit the brake shop. Tomorrow would be another day.

I did however press on as I removed, cleaned, tested and repainted the front shock absorbers. The rubber bushings were half worn, but if I couldn't replace them readily, I would use the old ones. The shocks seemed to be in excellent working order as demonstrated by the amount of muscle necessary to hand operate the movement.

I started reading Chilton's restoration book today, thinking maybe I could pick up a few pointers—it never hurts to see what someone else can offer. Also I got a book at the library on American cars. I found the story about Walter Chrysler very interesting. He started work with Buick in 1912, having been recruited by General Motors chairman James Storrow. Chrysler took a $6,000 per year cut in pay from American Locomotive in Pittsburgh to work here under Charles Nash (later of Nash automobiles). What was on his mind, I wondered.

As a production man Walter Chrysler managed to increase Buick sales tenfold, and his salary rose to six times his starting pay. Chrysler noticed early that workers were spending several hours finishing the wood framework for the inside areas of the car—parts no one would ever see after covering (except maybe a mechanic). It was partly by stopping this practice and other inefficient building techniques that he was able to increase Buick production so greatly. In 1916 Chrysler became president of Buick after Nash and Storrows left to build the Nash.

In 1920 Chrysler left Buick and accepted a $1 million a year job at Willys Overland. His spare time went to rescuing another company, Maxwell. In 1924 Chrysler made it clear to his associates that if Maxwell's new look was accepted at the New York auto show the new name of the car would be Chrysler (is there a connection here to the New Yorker?).

However, because his new car was not yet in production, the rules prevented him from showing it. So Chrysler rented the entire lobby of the Commodore Hotel and proudly put his prototype cars on display there where all the bankers and money men were lodging. As a result he secured the backing he would need to fulfill his dream. In 1925 Maxwell Company became the Chrysler Corporation. In July of 1928 the two widows of the Dodge brothers sold their company to the New York bank Dillon, Reed & Co. and Walter Chrysler snatched it up for a mere $146 million.

Chrysler immediately introduced a low priced car, the Plymouth, and second a medium priced car, the DeSoto, to accompany the Dodge. Chrysler was strong and healthy new company with its production admired. Walter Chrysler brought in designers of distinction and capable managers. But as with many car companies of that time, the vision and decisions of the founders provided the course.

When Chrysler died in 1940 the corporation seemed to level off at idle, losing the drive and motivation inspired by Mr. Chrysler until the rush of postwar demand.

Walter Chrysler had a strong influence on his designers, even after his death. If you ever wonder why the roofs of Chrysler cars are high, it is because Walter Chrysler believed that one should not have to remove one's hat while entering or driving one of his vehicles. Notice this the next time you look at an older Dodge, Plymouth, Chrysler or DeSoto. I have even seen several Chrysler advertisements in old copies of Saturday Evening Post and Life magazine that show people. They're wearing hats!

During the last two weeks of May the front brake drum fit was corrected at North Division Brake. Decreasing the shoe lining thickness by ⅛-inch total was necessary (¹⁄₁₆-inch per shoe). It seems that today's replacement linings are thicker than the originals, making it difficult to fit the drum. There are only two options for correction: (1) remove enough material from the lining to achieve a fit (result: less lining, less lifetime wear); or (2) remove material from the drum by turning on a lathe, thus increasing the diameter (result: less lifetime wear, less strength).

Because the drums measured nearly new condition and it seemed more expensive to replace them after a few turnings, I elected to reduce the lining thickness. Linings can be replaced more easily and cheaply than drums, not to mention the time to find new or usable salvaged ones. In the future when the linings need replacement thickness, I will investigate bonded linings rather than the conventional rivet type. I believe this method is available and not having rivets in the way of wear, it is possible to gain more life from the lining. During the weekend of May 18 and 19 the front brakes were reassembled and adjusted.

I received the new master brake cylinder in the afternoon on Friday, May 17. Because the new master cylinder was purchased off the shelf as NOS (new old stock) it was necessary to disassemble, clean and hone out a small amount of surface corrosion it had accumulated in the many years this item remained stored on the shelf. A small flexible wheel cylinder hone was adequate to perform the finish on this 1-inch bore. Persons not familiar with the art of honing should take note that one must constantly move the spinning stone in and out, never letting it remain in one area too long. The finished piece will have a dull, smooth, crosshatched appearance.

The pivot arm for the clutch and brake pedal were pressed out of the old master cylinder and onto the new. The brake line adapter was also removed from the new master cylinder and the old adapter was installed to facilitate connection of the hydraulic lines on my car.

This unit probably fit several different makes and the adapter was set for the vehicle/year intended. Not until later years after production ceased was it necessary to sell only by core part number, which is what the master cylinder itself was. Keep this in mind as it may benefit some part you are working on in the future that could require only a minor alteration to be useable. Most part suppliers have this information available.

The new master cylinder finally was installed onto Goliath without any anomalies. The entire hard line portion of the brake system was inspected and then cleaned with solvent and flushed with isopropyl alcohol, then reconnected. The system was now complete and ready for service and bleeding.

With Ginny operating the brake pedal we accomplished the bleeding process to remove all trapped air. We started with the right

The old master cylinder shown at the top in this photo was replaced because the corrosion inside could not be removed without enlarging the bore or resleeving it. A new master cylinder shown in the lower part of the photo was installed and all of the clutch and brake pivot arms were cleaned, inspected, lubricated and reinstalled.

rear as recommended in the shop manual, this being the furthest point from the fluid reservoir and thus able to remove most of the air in short order. The remaining sequence is left rear, right front, left front, finally ending up at the wheel closest to the supply source. Upon completion of the bleeding a pedal stop and master cylinder contact rod adjustment were done (this is again to obtain operating tolerance for pedal travel, much the same principle used in the rear end axle free play), followed by another bleeding of the system.

Minor wetting around the "B" nut (flare nut) connection of the master cylinder hard-line was observed, but not enough to form a drop. I made a mental note to monitor this connection for possible rework later. Now all functions of the hydraulic portion on the brake system were in working order.

With the brake work done for now, it was time to connect the driveline from the transmission to the recently overhauled rear end. I had already cleaned, sanded, wire brushed and repainted the driveshaft. The balance weights were still in place and I took extra care not to disturb them in the cleaning process. The rear universal joint looked like it had taken the brunt of damage during the rear end lockup. In fact by the looks of things it was easy to identify the weakest link.

I called Yarman Driveshafts and could you believe it, the shop had one in stock for $50. What luck! "Size-wise this is still a common part," the man told me. I ran down to his business with driveshaft in hand and returned home in less than one hour.

The front universal joint was in very good condition so I carefully took it apart, inspected all of the needle bearings, end caps, seals and casting, put it back together with wheel bearing grease and installed it onto the drive line.

Crawling now under the car to put in the driveline, I admired how all the work I had done so far was beginning to show progress. I even bought a case of flat black paint at a swap meet and painted over the undercarriage (12 cans, $15). It looked brand new. The only task left underneath was to reconnect the emergency brake.

This portion of the car had not been completed by Mr. Montrose upon replacement of the engine in 1972. On May 26 I started from scratch reconnecting it—a basket case! After the usual cleaning and wire brushing of all parts I used clear lacquer to coat some of the pieces that would otherwise corrode back to rust brown soon.

The first order of business according to the Chrysler shop manual was to ensure that no more than .005 inch end play on the transmission mounting arm and the hat section anchor bolt on the circle shoe was possible. Measuring, I found excessive play in the neighborhood of .040. The corrective action in the manual was to squeeze the hat section in a vise or lightly tap it with a hammer. The bench vise in my garage was not adequate to squeeze the material so I decided to tap on it with a hammer.

My first try was successful in reducing the gap some. I removed the circle shoe and figured if a little was good some more would be better. Using a heavier hammer this time, I began to see the gap close as I struck the hat section piece. I should have stopped there; a gain of .035 inch was all I needed and certainly what was visible came

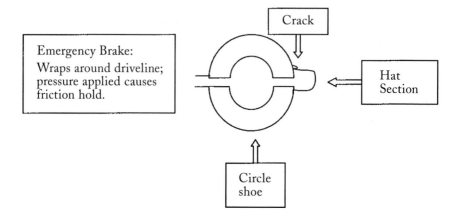

close. Oops! After several raps I noticed that I had cracked the hat section at the lower attachment radius. I struck out! I wouldn't complete the job today. The fix would require a weld—not easy to get done on a Sunday afternoon.

Oh well, what the heck, I had another half a day left. What could I do? Go and buy the battery, that's what. I was close enough now. Time to move on to the next job. Would the engine even turn over using the starter motor? Around 1 PM I removed the old Sears battery from the car and headed out. First a stop at Dave's Chevron station at the corner of Ave. J and Division St. The conversation with the attendant went like this:

"I need to load test this battery."

"Sure, no problem."

"It's from a 1948 Chrysler."

He stopped dead in his tracks, on his way towards the tester. He turned and looked at me, his eyes widened, he scratched his head and continued his pursuit. We connected the tester and found the battery completely dead.

Now, normally one would say, "You need a new battery." But this kid said, "Let's throw it on the charger for an hour. Nothing to lose!" Even though the battery was at least 20 years old, he was willing to attempt to breathe new life into it. Was it the mention of an old car? The Magic? Hell, the battery was older than he was. But I figured the magic was working again, and he wanted to help.

I went home, cleaned up the mess made earlier and put away my tools from working on the emergency brake. I returned to the station about an hour later to see the kid standing over the dead battery doing another load test. There was no way to restore its lost energy; the battery was shot. He looked at me with the expression of "We sure gave it a try." A very admirable try, I thought. I kind of knew in the back of my mind it would not work but the attendant's determination to try was commendable. What the hey! Three dollars to attempt a charge was cheaper than buying a new battery. At least for now anyway.

I headed over to Pep Boys, the closest place open on a Sunday that would have a 6 volt battery. (That's right: I guess I failed to mention before that Goliath was a 6 volt positive ground electrical system.) The salesman and I looked up the suitable replacement battery, but we didn't go over to pick it up until he told me about his Lincoln Zephyr he had restored. The part number was 0011345 and the price $28.88. The 20-year-old Sears battery was an acceptable core exchange.

3

Coming to Life

With summer approaching, the heat was starting in Lancaster already. On my way home with the new battery, the temperature/time display at the bank read 94 degrees. I got home and slammed a 24 ounce ice tea in one hit. Then I installed the battery.

Now it was time for a "smoke check." I learned this from an instrumentation engineer at work who always included it in his check-out procedures. The idea is to turn on the system and inspect for smoke before proceeding. I turned the ignition key (but not before trying all the other keys on the chain first—I realized this was the first time I had tried any key in the ignition). It felt good, turned easily. Clink, something contacted. I noticed the ammeter spring to life, needle indicating a slight discharge. This was good. I didn't smell anything, a walk around the outside turned up no problems, and everything seemed all right under the hood.

Okay, try the starter! At first it didn't do anything, Then all of a sudden it engaged and the motor started to turn over, a little faster each revolution. It felt like it wanted to catch. Within about three revolutions I saw the oil pressure gauge move some. Wow, this was great!

I had more to check out before actually trying to start the engine, though. Ginny was watching all of this from her sewing room window. When I got out of the car to look it over, she yelled

51

out "All right, baby!" Immediately, I grabbed my five gallon gas can and handed it to her as she came out to congratulate me. I gave her six bucks and she was off to the Chevron.

While she was gone I serviced the transmission (10W oil for a fluid drive). The torque converter is serviced from inside the vehicle by lifting up the carpet, opening a one bolt panel and rotating the engine until the service plug is visible through the panel. This is of course unless the larger floorboard plate is already off. The repair manual is very specific in warning the serviceman not to drop the plug into the bellhousing. I stuffed a rag around the area so if I did drop the plug it wouldn't go to the bottom.

I serviced the torque converter with the same Dextron transmission fluid used on modern Chryslers. I added plain water to the cooling system and rechecked the engine oil. When Ginny got back we both just stood there looking at each other while I poured gas into the tank. I saved a quart to prime the carburetor. One final mental check and there was no doubt. Judgment day had come. Yes indeed, I was walking around about two feet off of the ground.

I poured about an ounce of gas down the throat of the carburetor, holding the butterfly valve wide open with my hand. I shot a three-second spray of starting fluid (ether) in along with the gas. Yes, a carburetor cocktail. I climbed in behind the steering wheel. Switch on, the gauges all registered, I pushed in the ignition button and whammo! It started and then quickly died. I mixed another carburetor cocktail, pushed the button again and the engine ran about five seconds before it quit.

On the third try she ran for 30 seconds and built up 40 pounds of oil pressure then silence. I figured by now the gas in the tank should be getting close to the fuel pump, but the accelerator pedal didn't feel just right, probably due to the floorboard plate not being installed and properly connected.

I put Ginny behind the wheel and gave her some quick instructions as to where the ignition key was, what button to push for the starter and where the oil pressure gauge was. While I was doing this

I also glanced at the fuel quantity and it read a quarter tank. Wow. This thing was working and it hadn't had juice flowing through it for 20 years. Amazing how those electrons work.

I mixed up another nitro cocktail and yelled for Ginny to hit it. When she did the engine sprang to life and just idled there picking up each cylinder one at a time whilst I aided by jockeying the throttle. The smoke cloud out of the tailpipe put enough emission in the air that it was probably visible to one of our weather satellites circling overhead. I guess it was all that penetrating oil I had put into the spark plug holes back in February. I had to keep moving the accelerator control arm to keep the engine running smoothly, all the while looking up over the hood at Ginny sitting inside. She gave me a thumbs up on all of the gauges.

Shut it off, check it out, this can't be for real. We were both on cloud nine. This beast of a car had sat idle for twenty years in the Montrose family driveway, through heat, rain, snow, sandstorms and God only knows what else. All we did was add oil, water, gasoline and a little bit of electricity, and boom, the damn thing worked. What an incredible feeling. Zamboni was sure it needed lots more work but maybe my messing around with some of the wiring was part of the secret. Saul could never get it started back in 1972 after he replaced the engine.

The car was still sitting on all four jack stands with no wheels and tires. Then it hit me, what about the rear end? After all the work I had done, I hadn't tried the transmission yet.

I hopped in, turned the ignition key, pushed the starter button and she fired right up, this time without the aid of priming. I slowly pushed in on the clutch, grabbed the gear selector and dropped it into "Low Range"; it went in with a mild groan. I slowly released the clutch pedal. Holy scummolly, the rear drums were turning. I couldn't believe it—this was absolutely incredible. Turn it off, don't push it, I thought.

Time to celebrate and *thimk* (spelling left over from the 1960s). I asked Ginny to mix me a big 7&7 while I looked around. She was so happy too, it wasn't half a minute before she returned. The radiator overflow started to relieve somewhat and I wondered if it had gotten too hot. Oh, drink your drink, relax, you just fired up Goliath. I couldn't believe it. I have heard a lot of stories about people leaving old cars and tractors out in a field or in a barn for a long time. They would say, "All I did was pour some gas in it, give it a jump start and poof, away I'd go." Until today I always thought these people were stretching the truth a bit, but I was a believer now.

On Monday, May 27, I took the broken emergency brake band in for welding. The welding job was no problem and I picked it up on the way home. There wouldn't be enough time to install the brake band that evening because of other commitments we had. But I was so anxious to install the part that the next day I called in sick with what I termed Chrysler-itis. I was so thrilled it made me ill.

On Tuesday, May 28, with my new freshly welded emergency brake ring in hand, I proceeded to install the pieces for a second time. Because of this, that and the other thing I spent about six hours putting it all together. The whole cable assembly had to be removed, cleaned, lubricated and adjusted. It was about 3:00 in the afternoon when I finished. Sarah and Emily were just coming home from school and Dad was playing hooky (I didn't tell them of course). They were content to see me home so early and wanted to help. I still had to put the wheels on, downjack the car and drive it. We were expecting friends over for dinner, so I didn't have much time.

With the car sitting once again on terra firma, all parts installed and the lug nuts double checked, all of the tires required inflation. It was time to drive. I asked Ginny to get the camera, but she had to load film first. (Has this ever happened to you at an important moment?)

I hollered out to Sarah in the yard to see if she would like to ride. "Yes," she said eagerly, but when she opened the passenger door to get in, there was no way she was going to sit on that seat without first covering it. How picky girls can be about their clothes—even play clothes. I waited till Ginny found a seat cover for Sarah, settling for a white sheet.

Once Sarah was inside and situated, I put the car in reverse and we started backing out. I was too close to the brick wall on the right and too close to the flower bed behind. It took several attempts at moving forwards and backwards inching my way out of the hole I had placed the car in on that first day home back in February. Moving the car back and forth got to be challenging because I had not yet driven the car and the steering wheel was enormous and difficult to turn without power steering, a reminder of what some call "Armstrong Steering." We bumped the garage wall once while maneuvering because I thought we were in reverse when we were in first gear low range. Ginny got a little bit excited when this happened and loudly verbalized that I should calm down.

On the fluid drive shift selector, reverse and first gear, low range are virtually in the same location, the only difference being the placement of the linkage interconnect. The arrangement is similar to reverse and second gear on a conventional column shift three speed, or "three on the tree." My *Motor's Auto Repair Manual* had a good explanation of the operation of the fluid drive transmission:

HYDRAULIC-OPERATED TRANSMISSION
CHRYSLER & DESOTO 1946–51   DODGE 1949–51

Known as the Prestomatic Fluid Drive on Chrysler,
Tip Toe Shift on DeSoto and Gyromatic on the Dodge,
the actual transmission and hook up are identical on all
these cars.

All these units have a manual control (shift lever) for
reversing and for the selection of the forward speed ranges.
Two forward automatic speed ranges are provided. Shifts
are automatic between first and second and between third
and fourth ratios, but require manual shifting between low
and high ranges.

The gear shift lever has four positions: namely, High
Range, Low Range, reverse and neutral positions are
conventional, while high and low range positions occupy
the places of high and second in conventional three speed
gearboxes. All designs use a fluid coupling in conjunction
with a conventional pedal-operated clutch. Normally 98

percent of the driving, including starting, can be accomplished with the shift lever in high range.

With the shift lever in "high" or driving range the car starts in third, and at approximately 14 mph or more, momentary release (about one second) of the accelerator allows the transmission to shift automatically in high, fourth, speed. An automatic downshift from fourth to third occurs when speed drops to about 12 mph or less.

Shifting is accomplished by springs and hydraulic pressure; Supplementary automatic controls include a speed sensitive governor, kickdown and ignition interrupter switches, and a transmission-operated oil pump. The 1949–51 transmission is fundamentally the same type as the 1946–48 unit but its design and electrical circuit has been simplified.

Once we were free of all obstacles and backing down the driveway, Sarah looked over at me kind of happy and relieved and said, "Daddy, I have to go to the bathroom." As I waited, Ginny had got the camera loaded and snapped off one picture. We were straight and level in the street, Sarah now back inside smiling even wider.

I put the car in low range and released the clutch pedal and added normal accelerator pressure. Goliath moved forward. More accelerator and I glanced at all of the gauges; they looked fine. We were doing about 15 mph. Jerry and Frank, our neighbors to the south, were working in their front yards, and as Sarah and I drove by, they both smiled and gave us a big wave.

We came to the corner at the end of our street and I tried the brakes. Perfect, a slight pull to the left but nothing that couldn't be adjusted out later. We turned left and proceeded east on Nugent St. Left again on the next block but I couldn't get the transmission to shift up automatically, so I shifted to high range low gear. This worked and allowed a faster speed. A feeling of elation overtook me. Goliath felt just great, moving under its own power.

Smiling from ear to ear, Sarah pointed to the radio and asked if it only played old music. "No," I said "It will play whatever type music you choose." It wasn't the moment to explain how radios and amplitude modulation worked.

On the maiden drive of Goliath, Sarah and I take the second lap around the block. It soon became obvious that a new set of four shock absorbers would improve the leveling and the ride.

We rounded the corner again, as Ginny watched from the middle of the street and snapped another picture. Sarah and I cruised right on past her to take a second lap around. When we pulled back into the driveway Ginny showed tears of joy. I popped the hood. All was well as the overflow from the radiator vented off a bit. Welp, the maiden voyage was over. We were all excited but it was time to clean up for the barbecue.

When our friend Mike Bondy and his family arrived, I just had to take him for a ride. The girls opted to wait until the car was reupholstered before riding along. We hopped in and rode over to show off Goliath to Dan Bain, my friend who had helped me haul the original engine home. After we finished at Dan's we rode around the corner to Mike's house on Kettering St., then visited his next door neighbor Bruce who had a 1953 Chrysler Windsor. I wanted to check out his wiring to the carburetor and transmission relays. It wasn't the same, though, as I had read in the manual beforehand.

Mike and I borrowed his compression tester while we were there and returned to my house. The girls hadn't started dinner yet so we proceeded with the compression test, as the car was still warm. All cylinders indicated a compression pressure between 110 psi (pounds per square inch) and 120 psi with the exception of cylinders 1 and 4, which were 90 and 95 respectively. This measurement was very good, indicating an engine in excellent health. There would be no need to overhaul the engine.

I was very happy about that and took it as confirmation that the engine Saul installed back in 1972 was indeed a fresh overhaul. Although he had told me this, I had had my doubts about its internal condition considering the amount of time that had lapsed. Mike and I concluded that the lower compression of cylinders 1 and 4 was because these two cylinders were probably the ones with the valves partially opened while the car sat for so long. The result was more than likely a small amount of rust on the face of the valve seats, preventing them from sealing perfectly during the test.

ENGINE SPECIFICATIONS

Model: C39N

Type: 8 cylinder in line (flathead), valves in block

Bore x stroke: $3\frac{1}{4} \times 4\frac{7}{8}$ in

Displacement: 323.5 cu in

Maximum brake horsepower: 135 @ 3200 rpm

Crankcase oil capacity: 6 qt

Firing order: 1-6-2-5-8-3-7-4

4

Gathering Momentum

My next two priorities now that I had Goliath running were to get the transmission shifting and to complete the registration paperwork with the DMV (Department of Motor Vehicles). I found that because the car had not been registered since 1972 and the pink slip (Title of Ownership) had the identification number of the older engine (that's the way it was done back then), I would have to go to the California Highway Patrol office and have a person there verify or install a new data plate and vehicle number that could be used as permanent identification.

While we were all together eating dinner that night, Mike told me about Hiro's transmission shop on Avenue "I." They had a guy there named George who knew vintage car transmissions but charged $30.00 per hour labor. Mike said that George had really helped his brother out in the repair of a 1959 Ford truck.

Wednesday, May 29, I called Hiro's and made arrangements to drop off the car after work. George was a busy guy in a high production shop. He asked if I could leave it so that he could play around with it, spare time permitting. I took my chances driving the three blocks to his shop without any registration papers. Would you ticket a person restoring a '48 Chrysler?

Between May 29 and June 6 while the car was in the shop, I received a positive reply to a query I had sent *Classic Car Collector* magazine. I had written to the editor asking if he would like to buy the beginning story about Goliath as I had written in the journal I was keeping. His letter said he would be interested and for me to send my manuscript. I didn't rate myself as a literary genius as such, but I was trying different stabs at raising some money to restore the car. Here I had the opportunity to sell my story if he liked it.

On June 4 I obtained permission from NASA management to write the magazine article that might bring some extra dough my way. This permission business was a matter of red tape due to a law that only allowed civil service employees to write magazine articles outside of their jobs and not in conflict with normal duties. The appropriate signatures were received and I had the green light. But I still lacked the literary talents that would transcribe my diary into a manuscript for a magazine.

I sought out the help of Linda Faulhaber, the local NASA *Dryden X-Press* newsletter editor at that time. Linda agreed to read my diary and help. She was also interested in doing a piece for the newsletter called "All in the Family." After an interview at home followed by an interview at work and some pictures, the article "Rebuilding a Dream Come True" was printed and circulated throughout our work facility on June 14, 1991. This put the word out to several folks I worked with and I was able to gain a few more contacts and some moral support.

The short lived dream of writing a magazine article never produced any results. My story was too short at that time, and for one reason or another I never followed through. It wouldn't be until years later that I would be inspired to try again. Originally I thought maybe my diary could be passed to my grandchildren as some sort of heirloom to accompany the car.

On Thursday, June 6, I got a call at work from Hiro's transmission. George had managed in a week's time to get in about three hours' work on the car and wanted me to come in and drive it. He didn't say it was fixed. Meanwhile I had managed to get a temporary permit allowing the car on the road for test driving and a trip to the California Highway Patrol office. It wasn't free either; for a

30 day operation certificate I had to post all monies due: $75 tax, title, penalties and transfer. No problem, I was willing to pay whatever was necessary to be legal on the road.

Arriving at Hiro's that afternoon, I discovered that George had really not done much at all except read the shop manual and change a fuse on the kickdown relay. He had also adjusted the shift linkage, which was fine when I brought it in. We took the car out on the road while he explained what he had done. In reality it wasn't shifting any better; in fact, it still would not shift automatically at all. George was a very good transmission guy, but I realized this Fluid Drive system just wasn't every person's cake walk.

We returned to the shop and he said if I wanted to leave it longer he might be able to try again later in some spare time. I really didn't want to leave it any longer if he was only able to squeeze in three hours in a week's time. I was a little frustrated, too, because I had told George I thought it was a wiring problem and he had not attempted that direction except to change the fuse. I told George thanks, but I felt I could do more myself at home, having more time to devote to it. It would just take time to sit down, read and learn. George generously charged me nothing for his time and I proceeded to the CHP office and the DMV to finalize all the registration papers before I went home.

Work on the car didn't resume until the following Monday, June 17. The first item I learned from reading was how to go through a troubleshooting procedure step by step. I was reluctant at first to tackle a Fluid Drive transmission, but it was do or die—I had no extra bananas to spend.

I started into the procedure and arrived at the conclusion that it was the kickdown relay box at fault. I had to correct one problem at a time as they were encountered. I removed the relay box and cleaned it, inspected it, filed the contacts with crocus cloth and reinstalled the unit. I ran through the procedure again and it still wasn't working. The internal parts all seemed to be in very good condition, and it seemed to work okay with the Ohm's test and the touchy feely method. The windings did not show signs of burn, arcing or breaks.

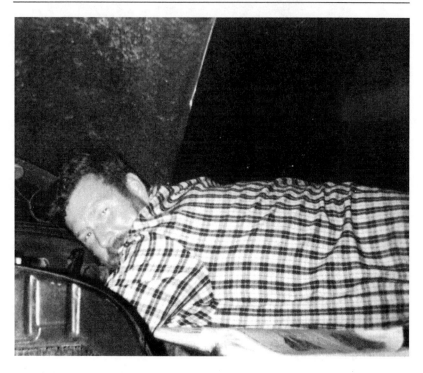

My first attempt at performing the transmission wiring circuit test procedure. The manual was close at hand as I learned.

The only next course of action would be to rewire the circuit externally and hope the problem could be the old exposed wiring shorting somewhere.

I don't know whether it was a godsend or the magic working again, but the next day at work I found that my friend Fred Ducane had returned to the Dryden Flight Research Center to complete another phase of testing for the F-111 Ejection Escape Capsule parachutes. Fred is a story unto himself. I had known Fred for probably six years or so, and the last time I saw him, I didn't think he would be returning to California. Fred worked for General Dynamics of Fort Worth, Texas. I knew him to be a very accomplished aerospace electronics technician and general spark chaser, which was just what I needed at this point. It wasn't that I didn't know anything about electrical work myself, but having an expert around certainly makes reading wiring diagrams, troubleshooting and fixing circuits a whole lot easier. And there's nothing like having a companion in the garage to tease and yell at or even vent off at once in a while. This is one area where guys understand each other, and Ginny, Sarah and Emily just didn't take my grease monkey sense of humor as well as Fred did. Have you heard the one about the man from Nantucket?

Fred and I had always had a good rapport. A very likable guy with much knowledge about vintage cars, Fred himself owned many cars including his pride and joy, a 1934 Cadillac. He had once worked for Chrysler, in fact. What a wealth of information he had! Right from the start when we greeted each other in the hangar, he demanded to know more about the progress I was making on Goliath. I had just purchased the car when Fred had left and his program was supposed to have ended. Much can be said here on the subject of collecting useful research data and the resurrection of completed programs.

Well, Fred was all charged up and couldn't wait to help. He told me his plans were to work on the car while he was here. His scheduled stay was going to be about four months, and he would rather come over to my house and help on the car in the evenings and weekends than stay in his hotel room or hang out in the lounge. This suited me just fine, so Fred and I mapped out the plan of attack we would pursue during his stay: wiring, engine and accessories.

He showed up at the house about noon on Saturday, June 22. I had finished all of my normal chores such as mowing the grass and sweeping the patio. I had rolled Goliath into the garage and was just about finished with repairing and readjusting the hood release and lock mechanism.

We discussed together the troubleshooting procedure in the shop manual and decided, since I had already taken apart and cleaned the kickdown relay, that the next step would be to completely rewire the transmission part of the electrical circuitry. We also took off the kickdown solenoid and the transmission governor assembly. These parts were an extravagant feature of the famous Fluid Drive transmission that made Chrysler automatic driving attractive to drivers of the 1940s who no longer wanted to be shifting gears. It was a prestigious thing to relax, enjoy and feel comfortable in a new Chrysler.

The contact points on the governor were corroded, and filing them smooth and square would provide proper operation. There was also some residual oil inside the governor casing to clean out. We replaced the terminal lugs and scuffed the contact areas to remove any tarnish. It didn't take long. At around four in the afternoon we were ready to try it.

We ran through the troubleshooting procedure again and this time the test light illuminated, just the way it was supposed to, step by step. Road Trip! We both hopped in and I started the motor. This was the first time Fred had seen or heard the car running. He looked over at me with a big grin on his face as I put the car in reverse and backed down the drive. He was silent and had his ear tuned to the sound of the engine. From his smile, one would think he had just placed first in a NASCAR event. Fred loved racing.

Driving at about 30 mph on Avenue "J" from 5th Street East on our way to Challenger Way, the car was not shifting at all. I was explaining to Fred all that I had done to the car and how concerned I was about the possibility of overheating. There was no way to read the engine temperature since the needle on the temp gauge had fallen off somehow. Fred looked over at me with an expression that said he had an idea. "Pull in here," he directed. We went into Buy N Save Auto Parts to see if we could find a temperature gauge to install temporarily. There was nothing there we could adapt or use on a makeshift basis. So Fred said to me, "Where can we get one of those meat or oven thermometers?" "Next door at Thrifty's," I said.

We purchased a glass meat thermometer for $3.85. Back at the car in the parking lot I noticed two people looking over Goliath and talking to each other about it. We opened the hood, relieved the pressure to the radiator, took off the cap, and stuck the thermometer inside the top tank. The temperature read 180 degrees Fahrenheit— not bad for a car that had been run, shut down and left sitting some 10 minutes with the outside air temp around 95 degrees. Fred told the folks admiring the car that he had a turkey in the trunk but it needed about another hour before we could take it out.

The temperature was perfect. Normal operating range was thermostat opening at 160 degrees and fully open at 180. I was happy and relieved to know that the engine would not overheat and cause damage. Next we got in and proceeded again eastbound on avenue "J."

We got about 200 yards down the road when all hell broke loose. The interior filled up with smoke immediately, and as I instinctively put the car in neutral, the rear wheels locked up and the rear end started bouncing and skidding. This all happened in about five seconds. Fearing the worst, I said to Fred, "I think the rear end has blown!" My mind filled with thoughts about all that work, all those hours gone to hell—but why? I coasted, or should I say skidded, my way into the center divider marked by two sets of double yellow lines.

What the heck was wrong? We were slowing down and I put the car back into low gear, just knowing that the hypoid gears in the rear must be just getting munched. I let out the clutch for one final moment before we stopped. But wait! We were moving again, and the car stopped skidding and hopping. There was still smoke, but we were rolling again. I glanced over my right shoulder to check for traffic and accelerated the car across the street to the right hand side of the road. The car was full of smoke, and it smelled terrible, like burning clutch. Fred and I got out, looked around but found nothing.

I was out in the street on the left side of the car walking around to the front when I looked inside the passenger compartment, and there it was, bigger than Stuttgart. The emergency brake was set! I had completely forgotten to release it when I left the shopping center parking lot. You see, two very peculiar things happened here at the same time. Number one, I'm not used to setting an emergency brake because both of my other vehicles have more modern automatic transmissions with a "Park" feature. But on Goliath, when you stop and turn off the engine, you have to set the brake or it will roll, even in a relatively flat parking lot. There is no "Park." I was not yet used to that.

Number two, what really happened of significance is that as I built up speed enough and paused, the car actually shifted automatically. We didn't even feel it. But what took place was that the emergency brake was not strong enough to hold the car in low gear as we started out so when the transmission upshifted to a higher gear, it produced less torque, allowing the now smoking emergency brake to take hold—and wham, the rear wheels started to do the jitterbug. Goliath had shifted automatically for the first time. What a ride!

I yelled over to Fred who was still looking around and told him what had happened. He looked at me real strange and said a few choice words about my lack of brains as we both got back in the car. I released the brake this time, put it in gear and we headed off again. I sure was glad not to have fried the rear end. Those few short seconds while that was all taking place felt like my mind and my ego degraded with warp speed. On the flip side now, I reflected on how lucky I was to have learned a valuable lesson without severe consequences. Think before you engage! New environment, new learning: develop a mental checklist.

Fred had to roll down the windows in the rear as we took off to get rid of the smell. I started out in low range first gear, got up to around 15 mph and shifted manually to high range. At about 25 mph, zip!, it shifted. Fred acknowledged my joy and announced loudly, "We're cruising now." I got the car up to around 60 mph, slowed down, then pulled off to the side of the road for another check of the water temperature.

We looked over the engine and all was well. It didn't seem to be excessively hot. I checked the pressure relief on the radiator cap and then removed it. Fred placed our newly acquired laboratory instrument in the mouth of the radiator and read the temperature. The water registered a perfect 160 degrees Fahrenheit. All systems go! I gave the engine area the visual once-over, closed the hood, and we got back inside. I made a point to release the emergency brake, then put the car in low gear, low range and proceeded back onto the roadway about 50 feet to the stop sign on 50th Street East. Left turn, 10 mph and it shifted again, but this time in low range. I was

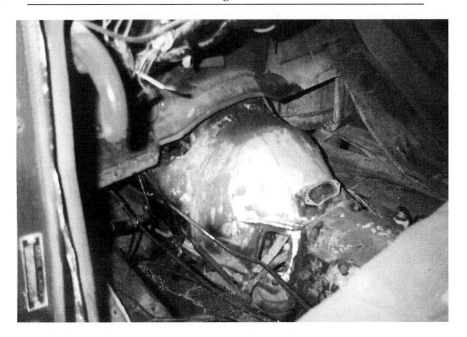

The large removable floorboard panel made it easy to access the transmission area. Note vehicle data plate on the left.

now cruising in high gear low range at about 25 mph. Then I shifted manually to high range and brought the car up to around 70 mph before I had to back off for the stop sign coming up at Avenue "I."

Alert now and proud that I had remembered to release the hand brake, at this speed I figured what a good opportunity to try a brake test. Hands off the steering wheel, I depressed the brake pedal with moderate pressure and had good brake action but still a slight leftward pull. I pumped the brake and the action got better. There still must be air trapped. I would have to bleed the brakes again when I did the adjustment.

As we approached a full stop I felt the transmission downshift. Another left turn but this time no automatic upshift in low range. I shifted manually to high range, got up some more speed and at about 45 mph it shifted up automatically. Two more times I did the same thing on the way home and was able to shift into high range, high gear: then on the third attempt I was able to get an upshift in low range to its high gear. Fred and I concluded that probably there was nothing wrong with the transmission, but that it just needed to exercise and have a chance to function under driving conditions. It was possible that some sludge had accumulated inside some of the oil passages, restricting flow.

We pulled back into the garage and Fred immediately got to reading the shop manual. I knew already, because I had read it earlier, that the upshifting was supposed to occur at 6 mph in low range or 14 mph in high range. Obviously the car still wasn't shifting the way it was meant to. Fred removed the ignition interrupter, and then the governor assembly and the kickdown solenoid. I pulled the service plug on the torque converter and checked the oil level there.

Fred was cleaning up the contact points again, talking both to himself and to me as he exclaimed over the value of such parts that the car had. All of the points were made of silver, he said. That's not what you get on a car these days. And the windings were solid copper, not just copper coated. We put the pieces back onto the car and headed out for another drive. It was still taking until about 45 mph in high range low gear to get an automatic upshift. I suggested that we knock off for the day; we had plenty of time ahead.

We popped a beer in the garage and did some serious head bobbing. Fred shared some of his stories from his days on the Chrysler test track. He exclaimed from out of the blue, standing with one foot forward and his free hand extended upwards in the air, "There's nothing on that car that's not fixable." I laughed and told Fred, "I think that's a word I've never heard before, *fixable*." But that was going to be the word for the day and a philosophy I would use from here on out. That was the end of Saturday. June 22, Fred's first day. I patted Goliath on the fender before turning out the light. It shifted today!

The next day, June 23, I was able to enjoy a few more rides around town before Fred and I approached our next plan of attack. Shifting was more frequent now, in fact every time, but the rpm required to achieve it was higher than it should be. We stuck to our theory that it was just going to take time to lubricate and loosen up the internal parts of the transmission. There might be varnish buildup or some other gummy substance that formed and had to free up with exercise.

A plan for flushing the transmission came about when Fred was reading the manual about diluting the engine oil in extremely cold climates with kerosene. This is what folks in the Midwest did before multiviscosity oils came into being. We also discovered a filter screen that could be removed and cleaned. Amazing what a little research and reading will do.

The removal of the filter allowed drainage of the transmission oil. There was a small amount of metal in the screen but normal in Fred's opinion. The oil should have been changed right from the beginning instead of just being topped off. It was marbled with dark brown, watery looking stuff. The new 10W oil I had in quart bottles had a golden sparkle. There was also a drain plug on the transmission itself. When I removed the plug just to make sure all oil was drained, I noticed the plug was magnetized and removed a small amount of metallic fuzz with the aid of a clean rag.

I funneled one quart of 10W oil into the transmission and Fred went to the parts store for some kerosene. When he returned I topped off the level with kerosene until fluid came from out of the fill hole. We jacked the rear of the car and put it on jack stands. I started up the engine, put it into low gear, released the clutch and just let the wheels turn with the engine idling. After a minute or so I placed the transmission in high gear and let it turn. When I put my foot on the brake to slow down the turning tires the transmission downshifted on its own.

Now when I pulled the drain plug everything came out black and larger chips had accumulated on the drain plug. Nothing to be alarmed about, Fred assured me. The mesh filter screen had a few small particles and after hand cutting a new gasket from bulk flat stock, I reinstalled the screen. The transmission was refilled, this time with all 10W oil, until it reached the filler hole. This is consistent with the shop manual service instructions. A tapered pipe thread plug without a gasket needed to be tightened carefully so as not to overtorque it and possibly induce a crack on the casing.

Judgment time had come once again. Sitting inside the car, still on jackstands, I put it into low range low gear, released the clutch, added some rpm, let up on the accelerator … and it shifted! I pushed in the clutch, pressed on the brake, selected high range, let out on the clutch, gave it what little accelerator was needed to get the revs up, released the accelerator momentarily, and was elated when it again shifted correctly.

If Fred could have done a double back flip he would have. I started clapping my hands before shutting it off. We jacked the car down and headed out for a ride.

Once out of the driveway, I put the car in high range, released the clutch and we slowly moved forward. I added a little power, backed off at around 10 mph and bingo!, we fulfilled another first. For the rest of the day we put on about 50 miles and did over a hundred stops and starts. Goliath never missed one shift. All we needed to do was to flush the transmission out. Happy, we headed home for dinner and watched a beautiful evening sunset in the back yard.

5

Making It Tidy

On Tuesday, June 25, Fred and I began work on the engine bay area. Ginny, Sarah, Emily and I were to start a long awaited family vacation on June 27. We were scheduled to be gone 18 days for a visit to Sacramento, Northern California, Oregon and then back down to San Francisco via the coastline. It was a promise I had to keep. Sarah and Emily were out of school on summer vacation and most of our overnight stops were staying with friends so the motel bills would be minimal.

Fred wanted to have something to stay busy with while we were away, so we started that night by removing the carburetor, ignition distributor, voltage regulator, horn relay and transmission kickdown relay. His plans were to take all of the components apart and clean, inspect, repair and just refurbish them to the best possible state. Fred also wanted the ignition-wiring conduit that lies on top of the engine. This unit houses all of the ignition wires and splits them off to their respective spark plugs in an organized manner.

What Fred really wanted to do was to clean the unit up, paint it and then hand paint the relief lettering "SPITFIRE" stamped on the top, which also included lightning bolts—three on each end. The conduit was to be colored black, the lettering red and the lightning bolts were to be gold. That would make the engine look bitchin,' Fred said. He left the house that night with a box full of goodies and $40 to cover anything he needed to buy, and I began to prepare for vacation.

A left side view of the 323 cubic inch Chrysler straight eight.

June was a very productive month and I am certain that the magic was partly to thank.

When I returned from vacation, Fred had purchased a rebuild kit for the Carter, Ball & Ball carburetor. He had meticulously disassembled, cleaned, inspected, polished and measured for accuracy all of the moving parts and put it back together. He informed me that the choke was of the electric type, so the initial cranking of the engine starter also engaged a circuit that set the choke.

Fred had also gone over the other parts he had taken with him in June. He explained how he had used a brass wire brush and cotton swabs to get into all the tiny cracks and crevices. Fred replaced the ignition points and picked up a new distributor cap at Jason's Vintage Auto Parts in Palmdale, the same place he got the carb kit.

The right side of the engine during the initial removal of various accessories. The ignition wires and the distributor and carburetor are removed.

He was on a first name basis now, making friends with Gary the owner.

We began work again on Monday, July 15. Fred and I decided to go for it this time. We started to get down to the nitty gritty of it all, tackling more of the engine. That night after a good home cooked meal from Ginny, we removed the radiator, generator, starter, and water pump, keeping all of the old belts and hoses for use as spares. When we put it back together all of the belts, hoses and such would go in new. During this process we also discovered a few misconnected wires here and there that we would fix later.

On Tuesday, July 16, I took the radiator into ABC, located on the corner of Beech Street and Avenue "I," on my way in from work.

When I carried the radiator into the shop the older gentleman working there knew right away I was restoring an older car. He asked what it was from and recalled having done many of these in the past. It has a *humongous* water tank on top and three rows of cooling tubes and fins. The younger guy at the shop thought it came off of an 18-wheeler. It would stay overnight and be wrought and pressure tested on Wednesday.

This front picture of the engine shown during initial teardown offers a good view with the radiator removed. This motor was purchased by Mr. Montrose in 1972 from a wrecked vehicle, and the owner told him the engine had just recently been overhauled. The red Chrysler emblem in the upper right of the photo was replaced in 1995 some time after the restoration was completed.

That evening, again after a good home cooked meal (that was part of the deal I didn't mention earlier: we would feed Fred and it would be home cooked meals, no fast food), we removed the horns and the intake and exhaust manifolds. All of the other linkages associated with the carburetor were taken off too. Fred had spent the earlier part of the day drawing up a list of parts we would need when we started to put this beast back together. He was able to pick up new heater hoses (marked

The hood was removed to make working on the engine easier. Then the old black oily undercoating was scraped off.

"Made in USA"), water hoses, a new thermostat, new freeze plugs, some high temp paint, and silicone spray for a total of $120. We spent the remainder of the night putting a final topcoat on some of the components he had reconditioned while I was on vacation.

The idea of the silicone spray was to saturate the exposed exterior rubber pieces of the car, mainly around the window glass. This treatment, according to Fred, would revitalize the rubber from loss of moisture, make the parts pliable and restore their luster. The plan was to make several applications per week, working it into the rubber with our fingers as we applied it. Looking back on this a number of years later, I can testify that this really worked quite well. I continue to apply silicone twice a year up to the present.

On Wednesday, July 17, the hood was removed today to accommodate working in the engine area. I ordered a complete engine

CYLINDER BLOCK WATER DISTRIBUTOR TUBE

The water distributor tube directs the flow of water from the water pump against the exhaust valve ports which are the hottest spots in the engine. The tube is located between the cylinders and the valve ports near the top of the cylinder block. Replacement of this tube requires removal of the radiator core unless the engine is out of the chassis for overhauling.

The tube should be replaced whenever the engine is completely overhauled. If the tube becomes rusted or corroded, overheating of the engine will occur due to failure of the water to circulate properly through the cylinder block.

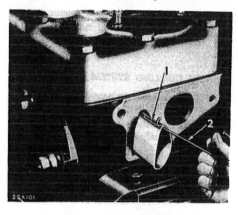

Fig. 20—Removing Cylinder Block Water Distributor Tube

1 Tube
2 Hook

overhaul gasket set from Terrill Machine Company in Texas at a cost of $75 (advertised in *Hemmings Motor News*). I did not plan to use all of these gaskets, such as the cylinder head and oil crankcase pieces, but to purchase a kit was less than buying the gaskets that I did need separately. In the future if I did need the others I would already have them on hand. I was certain to use the side valve cover, fuel pump, water pump, oil pump and oil filter cartridge assembly gaskets for a start.

I also ordered a water pump overhaul kit for $45 from Mitchell Motor Parts in Ohio (also advertised in *Hemmings Motor News*). I was very pleased with the service and shipment provided from these two businesses.

On Tuesday, July 23, 1991, I started the evening by cleaning up the engine oil breather cap, soaking it in cleaning solvent per the instructions of the shop manual. I set it aside to drip dry while I used my wire wheel to clean up the oil filler tube and associated brackets. I also polished the linkage rods from the carburetor.

Fred finished assembling the ignition distributor. Painstaking concentration I witnessed as he carefully masked off the distributor to paint only the necessary parts. The vacuum advance was not

With the engine components removed the long process of overhauling and reconditioning several parts is under way. Note the generator at middle right of the photo. In this picture I am reminded of the summer heat in the garage, broken only by the use of a fan. Ginny donated an old roaster pan which I used to soak parts in cleaning solvent and kerosene. Hardware on the cardboard, bottom middle, awaits a second coating of matte finish spray after it was cleaned and wire wheeled. My trusty repair manual was always close at hand for reference.

functioning correctly, according to Fred; the rubber diaphragm inside was too stiff. So we would be on the lookout for an equal or better substitute.

The gasket kit had arrived today, with all pieces accounted for and an extra item I was not aware of, copper spark plug crush gaskets. How cool! Also, I picked up the radiator on the way home from work. The guy at ABC rated it as being in very good condition. The bill was $25.

Once all of the accessories were taken off, the process of cleaning and painting the engine bay area and the engine block took several days.

Friday, July 26, I ordered four new shock absorbers from Kanter Auto Parts in New Jersey. I also ordered two decals, one for the oil breather cap and one for the oil bath air cleaner. The total was $87.

By August 10, the engine had been stripped down to leave only the block, head and oil pan untouched. I disconnected the front motor mount and jacked the front of the motor about 1½ inches to allow for enough clearance to install a water distributor tube. The manual stressed the importance of this item in cooling of the valves; if the tube were not in working order premature valve failure could result. When I had taken the water pump off the distributor tube had not been there (the second missing part).

Now, having obtained a 1¼ inch diameter brass tube the length of the engine with a wall thickness of .030 inch, I formed it into an oval shape with a rawhide mallet so it would fit inside a like hole located behind the water pump. It was necessary before installation to notch oval holes in the top apex of the tube so that water would exit these openings inside and direct water onto the exhaust valve area to provide cooling. The theory seemed logical enough to me and since it was also mentioned in the shop manual, I fabricated this simple part rather than take the time to find an original replacement.

In this photo, with the radiator and the water pump removed, it is easy to see the location of the water distribution tube. I fabricated my own replacement.

The engine block was scrubbed with degreaser, hosed off at high pressure, air dried and repainted with high temperature silver paint. (Some engines were equipped with a high compression cylinder head. According to my research these heads were identified only by their red paint. When I degreased the engine and used a pocketknife to remove some paint, there was no evidence that this was a high compression head.) I would continue the firewall preparation and painting later in the day. Next week our plan was to begin the buildup of the motor.

By the time of my next journal entry on August 19, 1991, several accomplishments had occurred. The cleaning, degreasing and painting of the entire engine area and engine block was finished on August 14. Fred and I began installation of the parts we had removed,

Left: In the beginning: the overhauled oil pump and fuel pump. *Right:* Piece by piece, step by step, the accessories are reasembled onto the engine. Just a few weeks prior, the parts were taken off to be reconditioned. Pictured here are the oil filler tube, the oil breather cap, the generator and the distributor.

nearly all of which we had disassembled, inspected, repaired, overhauled or reworked as necessary, then repainted.

Fred and I took the intake and exhaust manifolds along with some miscellaneous pieces out to Bill and Jenny Riedhart's house because Bill had offered us the use of his sand blaster. We took him up on it and of course I purchased some replacement sand and a little extra to pay him back. We painted the intake manifold with high temperature gray and the exhaust manifold high temperature white.

This was not original, but what with the advancements of paint materials since 1948, it was Fred's contribution to enhancing eye appeal when the hood was open. Fred had a philosophy of "equal to or better than." I couldn't argue.

The intake and exhaust manifolds, carburetor, fuel pump, starter, generator, water pump, oil pump, oil filler tube, oil filter cartridge housing and all electrical relays and regulators were finished and checked for

The water pump, intake and exhaust manifolds and carburetor.

operation. Now we reinstalled them using new gaskets or compounds. All of the hardware received a light coating of lube oil or antiseize compound on the threads during assembly. Every attachment bolt was wire wheeled to reveal the DPCD (Dodge, Plymouth, Chrysler, DeSoto) head markings and then coated with matte finish spray or clear lacquer.

On Sunday the 18th we installed a new ignition wire harness, the ignition coil, and the carburetor linkage, the latter of which we found to be of the 1950 type and not 1948. More than likely it had been changed over when Saul Montrose replaced the engine back in 1972.

In the afternoon on Sunday Fred and I seriously began to discuss the replacement of the wiring harness that came with the car. We looked under the dashboard and when Fred peeled back several inches of the loom wrapping, it all seemed just like new. It was flexible and very brilliant in all color coding, so Fred offered up this solu-

We were almost there now. The ignition wire harness is already installed in this photo and soon the cooling fan will be. Fred was proud of his hand painted "SPITFIRE" and lightning bolts. Notice the two tone paint of the intake and exhaust manifolds as well.

tion. Rather than remove the entire harness we would cut, match color and solder splice all of the new parts onto the existing loom. He assured me that no integrity would be lost and once the looms were wrapped again with vinyl tape, it would be the same as if the entire harness were replaced.

I was reluctant to do this at first, and for a while felt like I was being convinced by Walter Chrysler himself. But when Fred mentioned it was possible that he might have to return home without notice, I decided to go with his plan. It was agreed however that if any bad wires or cracking of the insulation was found that we would replace the entire run. Fred said, "I gotcha covered."

By the next day we had spent about 10 hours doing the wiring and the job was about one-third complete. By now I had also ordered and received from Mitchell's Motor Parts a new vacuum advance unit and some bulk material used for the seal on top of the radiator when the hood is closed ($29 and $9). The spark plug wire harness was purchased at Don's Auto Parts on Avenue "J" in Lancaster for $32.

Top: **Doesn't it look fabulous! This left side photo shows the reinstallation of all accessories, including the completion of our rewiring with all wire color coding kept original to the schematic.** *Bottom:* **A shot of the right side shows the air cleaner decals and new hoses.**

The past two weeks of working on this beast certainly had been no cakewalk. It was hot, sweaty, dirty and knuckle busting labor.

6

Back on the Road

On Friday, August 23, 1991, the day's events culminated with the most crucial milestone so far. After two months of down time and many hours of work, Fred and I drove Goliath on a second maiden voyage. We had spent six nights straight finishing the wiring and building up the motor. Now we both had a day off work.

Our first attempt to start the car revealed problem number one. The starter solenoid would not engage the motor. Upon pushing in on the starter button the solenoid would pull in and then immediately release. No rotation of the flywheel. After some reading in the book we discovered that the clevis rod at the end of the solenoid could be adjusted, a point we must have overlooked during the rework. We continued to use the starter by holding in on the plunger by hand with only moderate pressure to at least get the engine running. Since removal of the starter was needed to adjust the clevis, I elected to continue with our other work and do this job later.

With the output side of the fuel pump disconnected so that we could check its operation, I sprayed starter fluid into the carburetor. Through several attempts the motor would fire up but run only as long as the starting fluid supply would sustain it. No fuel was coming out of the fuel pump. I removed the gas cap and blew two big breaths of air into the fuel tank. Fuel started to flow from the pump at this point, so the line was reconnected. This time rather than use starter fluid I poured about half an ounce of gas into the throat of the carburetor, turned on the ignition switch and the car fired right up. The engine ran well for about two minutes. Fred was tweaking the fuel/air idle mixture when the engine just up and quit. We tried five more times pouring fuel into the carburetor but the engine would run only as long as that fuel supply lasted.

Either the fuel pump was shot or the filter in the gas tank had clogged up when I blew into the tank, pressurizing it. I removed the fuel line leading back to the gas tank and used shop air, blowing backwards into the gas tank. This is the recommended procedure in the Chrysler shop manual to clean the internal filter in the tank, along with removing a drain plug (forward right side of fuel tank) and flushing the tank with some more gasoline poured into the filler.

We reconnected and again the same problem. I removed the fuel pump and reinstalled the original one that came in a box Mr. Montrose gave us when I picked up the car's original engine. The motor started up and worked just fine. Fred completed all the idle and linkage adjustments. I shut the motor off, topped off the radiator, restarted the engine and continued with leak checks of the fuel, oil and cooling systems. Good oil pressure, and a test of all electrical systems with lights, horn and ammeter showed that the generator was functioning properly.

I had found an aftermarket water temperature gauge, so we compared its registered temperature with that of our old trusty meat thermometer; both indicated 180 degrees Fahrenheit. This temperature was satisfactory under the conditions of summer heat and idling in the driveway. No rise in temperature, leak checks complete.

After several start-ups and shutdowns, it was time to drive (by this time we were getting pretty darn good at working the starter solenoid manually). Fred seemed to think that only one horn was working and the one on the left didn't always blast. He removed the dome cap and sprayed some lubricant on the bellows, and when I pushed in on the horn button it sounded like an old train was coming out from behind the garage.

Fred and I both gave the car another once-over, top and bottom, then we headed out. It sure was a lot nicer now. Backing down the driveway I no longer had to jockey the brake and accelerator to keep it running. Now Goliath had a smooth, very quite idle, just like a factory setup. Gosh it did feel great.

I was straight and level in the street now, just like a few months earlier, but it wasn't the same car; it was better. I put the gear selector in low range, released the clutch and away we went. At about 10 mph I let up on the accelerator and got a perfect automatic upshift. As we neared the end of the street, I depressed the brake, and at almost a full stop it downshifted automatically, just as it was supposed to.

My mood turned instantly towards elation as it had many times before. We were back in the saddle again! I looked over at Fred and he just smiled. We rounded the corner for about another half block to the next stop sign. The car shifted perfectly twice in a row. As we started Eastbound on Lancaster Boulevard the car again responded, click, shifto-chango. I began to relax some now that things were working. I pushed in the clutch and pulled the selector down into high range.

Picking up speed as we cruised down the road, I monitored all of the gauges: water temperature now at 160°F, oil pressure 35+ pounds, ammeter charging 6 volts, fuel ⅛ tank. The speedometer was smooth and I was glad I had taken the extra 45 minutes to pull out the cable and lube it with white general-purpose grease. I backed off on the speed, pulled over and we both got out for a visual. Fred and I didn't even have to communicate what we were pulling over for.

When the car came to a stop we got out and instinctively started a visual inspection. Nothing wrong, just a minor weeping of the fuel pump fitting that stopped when I tightened it a half turn. The operation was very, very good. The transmission shifting problem we had before was gone. Driving onto 30th Street East we made a U-turn and headed back to the garage. With all systems working well my ego was at an altitude of 30,000 feet. Back in the garage there was not much to do after another shakedown except drive it some more.

Fred had mentioned earlier in the week that when we test drove it he wanted to run it out to about 90th Street East and have a beer at the Old Timer Bar. I tossed the keys over to Fred, which seemed like the appropriate thing to do. At about 1:20 PM we took off. What a ride! Just phenomenal. Stopping and starting, shifting and cruising. It was a nine-mile ride out to the Old Timer but it was like traveling across country. Things on the side of the road and things out in the fields had more intensity to me.

I had played the radio before in the driveway but this time when I tuned in the local AM station the first words that sounded over the 43-year-old speaker were "loves me like a rock." *Magic*, it hit me I was feeling fantastic. I patted the dash and said, "You know it." Fred gave me a quizzical look and shook his head.

I suggested on the way out that we visit the guy at Glendale Auto Salvage, the place where I bought the third member. It was close to our destination, so we stopped there first. I had told him the day I bought the unit that when I drove the car I would swing in, and he really appreciated our coming by. This mere courtesy assured a better price on something if I returned, but moreover it felt good to make another person's day.

When we arrived at the Old Timer it was closed. I ran next door to a small market and bought a six pack of Mexican beer. With Fred behind the wheel we headed back into town.

On the way Fred mentioned how much nicer the ride would be with a new set of baloneys (tires). I said to myself, Dave, go for it. At my house I grabbed the checkbook and the new set of shock absorbers that had been delivered and we were out the door. Fred followed me in his car in case we had to leave Goliath. It would be nice to order some original equipment tires, but what with the added cost and having to wait, I didn't hesitate long over the decision to buy ordinary radial tires off the shelf.

I had been dealing with the folks at Apollo Tire on Avenue "J" for a number of years, and I figured that if I bought four new tires from them, they would install my new shocks as part of the deal while the tires were being mounted. I had just spent some $325 there about two weeks earlier. I was right, Roger made me a deal on four new Riken brand 215 75 × 15 inch steel belted radials with a 60,000 mile warranty for $229. The shocks were installed at no charge, and the price included the usual federal taxes, mounting, new valve stems and computer balancing. Roger also would include free alignment if I could furnish the specifications. I wasn't sure about that but told him I'd take a rain check.

The interest that the old car caused when I pulled in was enough to reaffirm my conviction of *magic* once again. Everyone in the shop came over to look at it, even some of the customers sitting inside waiting. The special care that the guys in the shop gave the car was obvious as it was hoisted and the old wheels removed. I made sure that the young man taking off the wheels on the left knew what reverse threads were before he began with the impact gun. The job was only going to take about 45 minutes, so instead of leaving, I convinced Fred to go across the street where we could have a cool one. We never did get one of those beers earlier.

When we returned about half an hour later there was absolutely no other work being done in the shop. Everything was on hold. There were four people working on Goliath, with no fewer than eight watching, customers included. The old rubber was removed from the rims and the shocks were in the process of being put on.

The tire installation posed an interesting problem—the matter of seating a new tubeless tire bead to an old 1948 rim. I was about to learn a very interesting way of overcoming the problem of not being able to inflate the tire after mounting. The seal necessary to start inflation could not be accomplished, even with a special tool made for just this purpose. You may have seen it yourself—a large inflatable cloth covered tube is cinched around the center tread of the wheel and causes forces the tire bead inward.

Well, after several attempts this was not working at all; even the boss couldn't do it. A guy who was working with one of the shock absorbers came over, took the tire and rim off of the mounting machine, sprayed starter fluid in a circle inside the wheel, stood back and dropped a match. Boom, instant explosion and the bead was seated. He quickly doused the flame with a shop towel and proceeded to inflate the tire to the proper pressure, 32 psi (pounds per square inch). He repeated this on the remaining three wheels. Starting fluid is highly flammable and I don't recommend doing this yourself, but it was one of the tricks of the trade and worked quite well.

Once the job was completed and I started the car up to leave, one of the guys who helped work on Goliath asked if I could just hold off on backing out for a minute because he wanted to check it out while it was idling. The hood was still off and I must admit, the first impression was "cherry." The running engine was barely audible. Not something you see every day—cleaned, reconditioned, fresh paint and just purring like a kitten. Another guy standing around asked if he could sit in the back seat. I had no objection to this and when he reached for the door I heard him say, "Wow, suicide doors." Once inside he was sitting there looking over the interior and he hollered to his buddy standing outside, "Driving Miss Daisy."

It was time to do some more driving now. I picked Fred up at the house and we drove Sierra Highway, headed to Palmdale. I had promised Saul and Gertrude Montrose that I would come by and give them a ride when the car was complete. The car was far from being finished, but what the heck, I'd show the progress so far. When we arrived no one was home, but a neighbor came out when he recognized the car. He told me that Saul was home earlier and would be home again soon. But "only Saul," he said. I questioned him a little further and he said that he figured the two had parted, going their separate ways. Gertrude had moved out not long ago but Saul remained, and there was a legal notice in the newspaper of the pending divorce. Now that really blew my socks off. Stranger things have happened, though, I'm sure of it. Maybe I would learn more on that story later.

By now we had probably stacked up 40 miles or so and all was well. We decided to visit our friends Bill and Jenny, whose sandblaster we had used, but they weren't home either. We were out on the rural parts of town anyway, so we decided to just cruise around. Our confidence level in the motor and accessories was strong at this point. Fred brought out his portable CD player and we headed out through the back country of the West Antelope Valley listening to the Black Crowes and Led Zeppelin.

On Avenue "I" and 70th Street West we pulled over for a scenery break and a look-see of the moving parts not visible from inside. Everything was looking good, except that the weep on the fuel pump had started up again. I asked Fred to wiggle the fan to check out the bearing on the water pump. It seemed loose to me, and he agreed. It wasn't leaking, though, which surprised me. Not a show-stopper but I would have to look into replacing the seal.

We continued to Avenue "H" then started towards the freeway. The new tires really made quite a difference in the ride. I let go of the steering wheel and the car tracked straight. I didn't feel the need to align the wheels but I would definitely keep an eye on how the tires were wearing. The day ended with a gorgeous sunset and around 60 miles accumulated on the well-oiled machine.

7

More Work to Do, and a Farewell

Now the car would have some down time again, and I generated a list of things to do:

1. Repair starter solenoid
2. Fix fuel pump leak
3. Repair water pump
4. Fix brake lights
5. Check tightness of all hardware that was recently put on
6. Adjust left front brake
7. Check tailpipe and muffler clearance against body; something was rattling sometimes at stops
8. Check emergency brake for adjustment
9. Shake down undercarriage
10. Take the family to the fair

On Sunday, August 25, I did no work on Goliath but instead decided to relax for a while and just spend some time with Ginny and girls. Everyone here at home had been so patient and caring. It seemed that most of my time lately had been spent in the garage. The girls liked coming out and helping sometimes. Sarah was a darn good gasket scraper, and I wondered if she comprehended my explanation of how engines work and the four stroke process (intake, compression, power and exhaust). I tried to explain how brakes work but she asked how come cars didn't use brakes like the ones on Mom's bicycle. A discussion on different designs ensued. Both of the girls loved to hammer and paint and nail things, so sometimes I would give them a piece of wood and a handful of nails and let them spray paint their creations. Sarah soon started adding wire and string to some of her projects.

Our niece Jessica had been visiting for the past week and I hadn't made much time to spend with her since her arrival. Ginny and I agreed that it was a perfect time to shut down all happenings at home. We loaded the whole gang into the pickup truck and headed off to the fair for the rest of the day and evening. The smell of corn dogs and cotton candy and the noise from the carnival rides kept my mind off of the water pump, which concerned me. I had the choice of two water pumps while we were building up the motor. One seemed loose while the other checked better in overall feel and appearance. However, upon driving some and attaching the belts I wondered if it was in such good condition after all.

The next day, Monday, August 26, I took the spare water pump to work with me and pressed the shaft out during lunch. At home that afternoon I rebuilt the pump from a kit I had purchased previously in anticipation of overhauling the one pump I did not use, thinking I would have a spare for future use if needed. That time had come all too soon.

That evening I removed the radiator, the fan, and the loose pump and installed the rebuilt one. As it turned out the fix was no good. The pump leaked water profusely from around the seal and the shaft. Both pumps in my possession now were unsuitable to run on the car. What was I to do? I was not about to run the risk of destroying the radiator if the pump failed, causing collateral damage. I certainly could not leave a leaky pump installed either.

Not much more work was accomplished for the remainder of this week. We had two flight days scheduled and I went to work early both days. Doing two 12-hour days on the flight line in the middle of the desert in August is enough to drain anyone's energy. I did manage to get another water pump on order, though—a superb deal at Kaos Auto Parts, $65 with exchange. It was supposed to arrive Friday the 30th, but when I showed up I was told there was UPS delay and I should check back September 3, the day after Labor Day. I was facing a three-day weekend with no water pump. Worse yet, the car was otherwise ready to drive and I wanted to drive it.

Although it had been a long and busy week at work, my coworker Wayne Copeland and I agreed to work this Saturday the 31st in order to turn the airplane around for the next week of rigorous flight testing the following week after the holiday. As it turned out, there was a great advantage in volunteering to work this Saturday.

When the water pump did not come in on Friday, that night the thought occurred to me that I had two pumps, each with different critical faults. What the hey, why not put the two together? I had nothing to lose except time, and with a three-day weekend ahead, time I could afford. And the press I needed to use was next to my rollaway toolbox in the hangar. How convenient! Saturday afternoon when all of the airplane work was done, Wayne and I went to work on the two pumps. I removed the shaft, seal and impeller assembly from one pump and pressed it into the pump housing containing the new bearing from the rebuild kit.

When I got home I installed the Frankenstein pump and voila!, a perfect fix. No leaks, no wiggle. I worked off some of the other items on the list like brake adjustment, brake light, hardware check, tailpipe and the emergency brake. Fred showed up early in the evening and we cruised around some till we stopped by Mike's house. Mike was home watching the kids when we stopped by to do another compression test using Mike's tester. A second test after accumulating 100-plus miles brought pleasing results:

Cylinder	Compression (psi)
1	110
2	115
3	115
4	130
5	125
6	125
7	125
8	135

After successful completion of the compression test, Mike wanted to go for a ride, so we piled three kids and Fred into the back seat of the car and away we went. Upon our return to Mike's house he shared his most recent work on a 1930 Harley-Davidson. Fred and I continued our cruising that night until 2 AM with all systems working very well and no anomalies.

The weekend driving and the Frankenstein water pump worked so well, I decided to drive Goliath into work on Tuesday, September 3. Whether this was just to check it out or to show it off I'm not sure. I drove in by myself so as to not inconvenience my carpool mate Wayne Copeland in the event something were to go wrong. Wayne had young ones at home and he and his wife Robin ran a close schedule.

The ride was great and the early morning chill held the water temperature at a steady 160°F. People on the road to work were mostly passing me today, as I was only driving Goliath at a safe 55 mph and most people on the road averaged 65 to 70 mph. Every so often people passing would wave or give a thumbs up. This made me feel good and my chest welled up in pride. One particular lady passing me seemed especially excited because she was honking, waving and clapping her hands. I got the impression from her joy that she might be an old car enthusiast herself; she sure was flailing about.

When I arrived in the parking lot at work everyone noticed Goliath. The gate guard seemed to add a little flourish as he signaled me past. Several folks came over to my work area throughout the day to comment on the car. At around 10 AM, Artie Hartington, Joe Kinn, Phil Marsh and I took the "Time Machine" for a ride around Edwards Air Force Base. All enjoyed the ride as evidenced by their comments. Phil kept on telling me how his Dad and his uncle both had Chryslers when he was young. In fact Phil himself had a new Chrysler convertible in the very parking lot we took off from. I had also slipped a 1948 copy of *Life* magazine in the back seat and Artie commented on the special effect it added to the drive.

The week passed by without any problems and many more fun filled miles stacked up. I tucked in some old sheets to resemble seat covers and took Ginny, Sarah and Emily on some drives around town in the evenings. We also drove the freeway up to the Palmdale Pass lookout point.

On Sunday night September 8, Fred and I decided to take a drive and wound up in Quartz Hill, so we again stopped by to visit Bill and Jenny Riedhart. Fred didn't know a lot of people in the Antelope Valley, but he and Bill just clicked when it came to personalities. A six pack was in order and a drive in Goliath for Bill and Jenny. We headed over to the drive-in dairy close to their house. On the way back I put Bill behind the wheel and Jenny up front sitting next to him. I instructed him on operating the Fluid Drive transmission from the back seat. Even with Bill's enormous beard I could see him smiling from ear to ear as I watched his expression in the rear view mirror.

We left their house at about dusk. Earlier I had noticed the amp gauge at full charge and not coming back to normal, as it should have once the battery charged after starting the motor. Fred and I decided to drive some further to check this out. As we proceeded the car started running rough and I caught a whiff of an overheated radiator smell. I looked down at the temperature gauge and it indicated well over 200°F. I immediately pulled over and popped the hood, and by now steam was everywhere. The smell of hot water and antifreeze is unmistakable. It wasn't until the breeze carried away the cloud of steam that I noticed a big gaping hole in the side of the engine block, right behind the oil filler tube. Luckily it was only a freeze plug that had let loose and blown out.

Fred jumped right on my case about doing a gravel road burnout when we left Bill's house. I could only assume that the water pump had put out some hellacious pressure when I revved the motor and dumped the clutch. It was enough to loosen the freeze plug and then the rising temperature just blew it the rest of the way out. Now there we were out in the middle of the desert, broken down. We stuffed a rag in the hole let it cool off, then ran another two miles before the motor started heating up again. We decided the rag would suffice to get us home, which was about another 10 miles, but we were going to need water.

Fred flagged down a passing car, caught a ride to a phone and called Bill. The guy gave Fred a ride back to where I was and in 10 minutes Bill and Jenny showed up with 10 gallons of water. We filled the system up and were only getting a slow drip from where the rag was stuffed into the hole. Bill and Jenny followed us home to my house while I humbly listened to a lecture from Fred all the way home about treating the car with more care.

The temperature never went above 160°F and two days later when I finally had time to start working on the repair, the rag was still holding water in the engine. About half of its capacity, I estimate, was relieved when I pulled the rag out. Fred was right and I promised myself never to do another burnout. I must, however, interject here that the freeze plug blowout was probably due to imperfect installation.

If you are familiar with old style freeze plugs, you know that they have improved significantly in their design since 1935, when this engine first went into production. The freeze plugs on a 323 cubic inch straight eight flathead engine resemble a convex silver dollar. The engineering is such that when one installs the plug the idea is to flatten out the convex side by hitting it with a hammer. In so doing the metal to metal friction holds the disk in place as the hammering enlarges the plug's diameter.

Thus, it is my conclusion that when I replaced these plugs during our engine downtime, I neglected to flatten them enough to achieve a perfect fit. Thinking back now and not trying to make excuses, I suspect that my experience with hammers and hitting things on this car, such as the emergency brake, may have made me a bit hammer shy. Still, I should not have been pushing the car so hard to begin with. Another lesson learned.

I replaced the freeze plug and added a bead of high temperature sealant around the exterior circumference. I also began to carry an extra freeze plug in the trunk, and I bought one of those expandable emergency ones, just in case. There are also two one-gallon jugs of water in the trunk if the need should arise. The amp gauge needle was still showing full charge, all the time. I pulled the generator and the voltage regulator to bring them in for a bench test. Fred and I could only determine a bad regulator with the multimeter I had in the garage, but we weren't sure that it couldn't also be a bad armature on the generator. Well, it was both. When I set the generator on the bench and removed the rear band type inspection cover, there was solder splattered all around inside. This is an indication of excessive heat, overworking the internal parts, most likely caused by worn bushings.

On September 12, I took both generator and regulator to Auto Parts Unlimited on Avenue "I" in Lancaster. There was a back shop located here that specialized in electrical components. John rewound the armature and I purchased a replacement regulator at the front counter. I was amazed at the parts still available locally. It took about a week and a half to get the armature done. By then Fred had gotten the news he was ordered back to Fort Worth, Texas. His company had decided that since it would be another month before the test article could be dropped again from the NASA B-52, the team should be called home. Actually this made Fred very happy because he had been out here since June and was starting to feel homesick, worried about his house and his cars. The plan was to come back out again when all was ready to fly.

I sure hated to see Fred go. We had spent a lot of time on the car and we had lots of fun in the garage. The news of Fred having to leave came fast while the car was down. We sent Fred off with a good old-fashioned barbecue. He loved eating steak and I slow cooked an entire London broil just for him on his last day in town.

8

Making It Shine

Goliath was back up and running soon, and now I was enjoying the car in longer spans as I tried to save the money to proceed with the restoration. I was facing the next three most major and costly parts of the restoration.

In October Goliath went into preparation to be painted, reupholstered and graced with a shining new set of rechromed or polished-up trim. The first estimate I received was while I was test-driving to check out the operation of the new voltage regulator and the generator. I kept shopping around for several weeks.

Bob Vasquez, whose upholstery shop was located on Avenue "I" near Beech Street in Lancaster, proved to be the most affordable of the three shops that gave written bids, not to mention the many guesstimates that others quoted. Bob's estimate for complete upholstery for $1600 was much lower for the same fabric and amount of work as two other local shops, whose prices were $2400 and $2900. I chose Bob's offer. The cost was to include labor and materials for all new carpet and reupholstery of the seats, side panels, armrests, headliner, windlace and kick panels.

The color I chose was gray on the side panels and headliner, light blue for the carpets, seat and armrests, and light blue matching carpet for the kick panels. The carpet would be made with a rubber heel pad glued and sewn into place. The carpet in the front

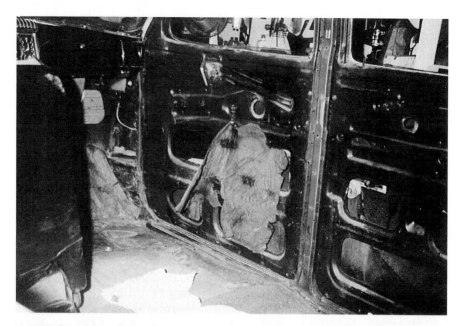

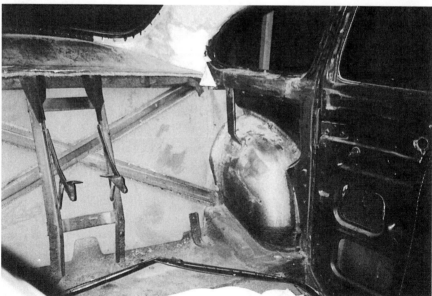

Top: After many fun-filled miles and a few setbacks, the time had come to embark on the next steps. *Bottom:* The rear of the interior with carpet, seats and door panels removed.

would be held in place at the forward end with Velcro so it could be pulled back when needed to service the brake master cylinder and the transmission fluid drive. My choice of fabric was a newer type composition of 50% cotton and 50% polyester.

Bob would recreate all of the original pleats and seams to maintain the same style. The door panels would be two colors, blue on gray, patterned after the original. I would have liked to have reupholstered with wool and mohair, but the material was far too expensive and even if I did the job myself I don't think the end result would have cost much less in terms of time, materials, and experience. Again an old adage taken from the vocabulary of Mike Bondy: "You can always do it yourself for just a little bit more." As far as the looks go in comparing the original to the new, I would say only that a points judge would rule against it.

Next came the paint and estimates. For this critical work I chose Al Simperson, a local who advertised in the *Desert Mailer* newspaper, the same paper in which I had found the ad for Goliath. The name of Al's shop was Adonai which is the Jewish word meaning the Lord. Although his shop was located in an industrial park in Palmdale, Al's overhead was such that he could do work for less. Couple that with the fact that he was just starting a new business and I got body work, body prep, primer and exterior painted to include inside trunk and door jambs for $1500. My other estimates around town were $2800 and $3900.

The weekend of October 19 and 20 I began to carefully and methodically remove all of the body trim: chrome moldings, stainless steel parts, bumpers, mirrors, hood ornament, spotlight, head and tail lamp bezels, sun visor, license frame and stop light. I identified each part in a handmade sketch, knowing that any identifying mark I made on the part itself could be lost during polishing and chrome plating. Some molding pieces used spring clips and others were held in place using a threaded stud.

The front waffle pattern grille separated into seven different pieces after it was removed first in one piece. I was amazed at the engineering and craftsmanship that must have gone into producing the

One of the first pieces taken off in the body and paint prep was the sun and snow visor. This beautiful option added so much character to the lines of Goliath, I had a hard time getting used to it not being there.

three metal castings that made up the outermost portion of the grille. They are positioned under the headlight and wrap around the fender to the rear. These pieces are not just a half circle in shape; a close examination actually shows a graceful compound curve with two distinct steps tapered to a point, much like a piece of wood with a routed edge. The casting of a part like this was an absolute marvel.

Also I took special notice of the rock and gravel guards. Evidently these were a development from the manufacturer's past experiences or an option added to more expensive vehicles. The forward lower corner of each rear fender is protected from paint chipping by a chrome metal sheet, apparently because so many roads of the 1940s weren't so well improved that the front tires wouldn't kick up rocks and this area was prone to damage.

I then turned to the interior, where I began to remove the seats and to strip the remaining items of upholstery. I took extra care in removing the door panels and the headliner so that Bob could use them as patterns to construct new ones. Bob had said he would do this but I figured what with the special deal I was getting I would go ahead and help. When I removed the back seat, I found under it a 1964 nickel, a Smokey the Bear badge, a crochet needle and a small lapel pin.

The paint and upholstery was going to be done in two steps. First would come the bodywork and painting of the

Next came the grille and front bumper. It was as if I were a dentist removing the mouth and all of the expression.

trunk, doorjambs and a portion of the underside of the hood. Then the car would go to Bob Vasquez's shop to install the upholstery, headliner etc. After that the car would return to Al's shop to paint the exterior of the car.

I delivered the car to Al very early on a Saturday morning, October 26, when there was no traffic. I phoned him at home and he met me at the shop. I drove Goliath bare bones—no bumpers, no mirrors, nothing but a shell with the license plate wired onto the

Nearing the completion of the chrome removal, Goliath seems to have taken on the appearance of a demolition derby entry or a jalopy racer. Note in this photo the position of the three wraparound chrome pieces that used to form the outermost part of the front grille. These are the ones that struck me as being exceptional castings.

trunk. We secured the car inside and both went home after Ginny arrived to take me home.

I was informed at work several weeks earlier by our crew chief, Joe Misplay, that beginning Monday next week we on the crew were to report for work not at Edwards Air Force Base but at Plant 42 in Palmdale, where we would work on the X-31. The X-29 program had completed all major testing and we were to begin familiarization with the operation and maintenance of the X-31 at the Rockwell B-1B plant.

This suited me just fine; in fact I couldn't believe how things were working out. It had to be the *magic* that was playing a part in

Here the rear of the car shows paint that was protected from sun and oxidation by the chrome brake light fairing, license plate and Chrysler emblem.

this. Why? Well, with Goliath now in Palmdale and possibly going back and forth to Lancaster, what else could it have been? I was going to have time to work with Al on the progress more often and it would be on my way to and from work or at lunch instead of in the other direction. Under our agreement to minimize the price of labor, Al was going to use my job to fill in the gaps with the rest of his work coming into the shop.

He used a 5-ton bottle jack and a 4 × 4 piece of wood, holding it in place with his feet, while he laid on his back inside the car to push out the dent in the roof. Incredible how it formed back to shape with hardly any signs of the damage ever being there. Al knew just where to apply the right amount of pressure. Al assured me the slight mark around the perimeter would disappear once it was primed and sanded. He was right.

107

Inside Al's shop, Goliath awaits two-part primer coating after the bodywork is near completion.

As I mentioned before, all of the fenders had some sort of damage and there were creases caused by the rear doors' having been opened too far at some point in the car's past. This is a common occurrence with suicide doors, and is one of the reasons we no longer see suicide doors on new cars. If the doors are opened while the car is in motion, the doors are easily blown open past their limits. Al worked meticulously with a body hammer and a dolly to smooth out all of the dents perfectly, using only the slightest amount of body filler. Astonishingly, none of the chrome pieces sustained any damage from when the rear suicide doors had sprung. I had to disassemble the right rear door post hinge at the attachment to replace a worn rubber stop. The stop was supposed to keep the door from ever contacting the car body. I used two rubber grommets that I found in my garage goodie box. The fix prevented the door from going beyond its stop limit and worked as good as new. The primer used on the car was a two-part epoxy filler type, according to Al. It was applied and allowed to cure.

Fred returned from Fort Worth on October 21 and was expected to stay until after Thanksgiving. This time he drove back to California in his own car and while Goliath was elsewhere we spent some time working on his Cadillac Sedan Deville.

Top: After a very hairy ride home from Al's shop, I photographed the completed trunk paint. *Bottom:* The door jambs and all areas that required paint prior to installation of the new upholstery were sprayed after Al had finished the bodywork and applied the primer coat.

The underside and unseen areas of the hood were sprayed prior to the exterior finish paint job.

During this time I also ordered several other restoration items that would enhance the finished car. I purchased from Steele Rubber company (advertised also in the *Hemmings* issue Artie had given me) a new rubber cowl vent seal, numerous other rubber bumper parts that attach to the body of the car in different places, a new rubber seal for the trunk and the rubber pads that fit under the chrome taillights and stoplight.

I drove Goliath home from Al's shop after the bodywork, primer, and painting of the doorjambs and the trunk. This drive was as risky as when I had delivered it. The car was just a shell with no bumpers, grille, headlights or chrome installed, only this time the car stood out even more like a sore thumb because of the yellow shade of the primer.

I waited until around 6:30 in the evening when hopefully there would be the least amount of traffic. I used as many back roads and streets as possible to avoid being spotted by patrolling law enforcement. I was certain that if I were to get pulled over I could sweet talk my way, but just in case, I tried to reduce any likelihood of detection.

On the way home it was easy to see the deterioration of the channel grooves that hold the windows in place and seal the interior from dust with the windows rolled up. They also act as a guide or a track for the window when it is rolled up or down. The fuzzy substance was worn off in some places and the thought occurred to me that while I was at this point of the restoration, it was worth replacing these in order to do a professional job. This was not in Bob Vas-

I spent several hours in the weekday evenings meticulously hammering out all of the small dings in the beauty rings, just to get them perfect. This photo shows the stages of repair: hammer, prime, more hammering, prime the finish.

quez's area of expertise, so I called around town to a few glass shops. The only one that I could find that had the parts to do the job was Healy Auto Glass on the corner of Lancaster Boulevard and Yucca Avenue, in Lancaster. Fred called these channels "cat whiskers," by the way.

The estimate at Healy Glass was $275, labor and materials. The guy there was friendly and even offered just to sell me the channel grooves if I wanted to do the job myself at home. It didn't seem that difficult, but after a conference with Fred I decided to bite the bullet. I'm glad now that I did, too, because during the process the right rear window got cracked and the replacement was free—a risk they assume when taking on a job. A new glass was cut and the job was completed. I figured if it had happened to me, the replacement window alone would have run into the neighborhood of $100 to purchase and install.

I spent the weekday evenings buffing and polishing some of the interior chrome parts, including the rear interior light bezel, the interior light switch cover, and the strips that attach to the interior doorframes. These also have a cloisonné emblem of a crown on them.

I removed all of the chrome radio knobs and polished them using 000 steel wool and chrome cleaner. I did the same process on the dashboard chrome and the interior door handles. The steel wool worked quite well. The door frames did not need to be repainted as a good cleaning left them looking as good as new. I was able to clean and polish up the chrome parts of the rear view mirror, spotlight and fog lights. These items were in such condition that they would not require new plating.

The license plate brackets, fog light brackets, sun visor strut and a few other pieces I prepped and repainted with gloss black spray paint. The hubcaps were also cleaned and polished and would not need plating. I used enamel gloss black paint and a small brush to renew the Chrysler lettering on the hubcaps. I reconditioned the rubber door mat sills with silicone spray after a good scrubbing with powdered cleanser. They looked brand new, as did the other parts.

All of the remaining chrome and stainless was to be done by Décor plating in Hawthorne, California, for an agreed cost of $1000 for stripping and replating of the chrome and polishing of the stainless steel. I had called and visited several shops in and around Los Angeles County and the best bid price I could get before calling on Décor was $1800.

I was at a chrome plating shop in Long Beach when another guy there saw me inventory the parts. He too was shopping around for prices to chrome some boat pieces. He came up to me after I received the estimate and handed me the card of Décor plating, saying he had just come from there and could find no lower bids. Off I went to Décor.

I laid out my pieces: two bumpers, five bumper guards, the seven piece waffle grille, the six wraparound strips I mentioned before from the grille, two rock guards, the hood ornament, two taillight housings, the brake light fairing, bumper bolts and all the trim and remaining molding. At first the estimate was $1300. I explained that I couldn't afford that much, I was in no hurry and possibly I could send a lot of business his way from the Antelope Valley; would he do it for $1000? He hesitated and said it might take until Christmas when business got slow and that he also wanted to train a new person. I said that was fine with me. We wrote up the invoice, I left a $250 deposit and home I drove. Simple as that.

My mother passed away November 15, 1991, and needless to say my spirits were low for some time. For several moths I neglected to record any entries in the journal I was keeping of Goliath's restoration. From early November until the middle of December Bob Vasquez had the car at his shop. The upholstery took quite a bit more time than Bob had anticipated, but the old car sitting there, just waiting for a new covering of cloth, worked its *magic* again and made him put in the extra effort to produce top-quality results.

Eventually Bob called me and said it was done. What a wonderful sight to behold! I continually get compliments and for certain the $1500 investment was well worth the $2500 or $4000 quoted by the other two shops in town.

I picked up all of the chrome for Goliath on December 15. The trip there was profitable too in that while I took Ginny and the girls to see *The Nutcracker Suite*, I managed to circle down to Hawthorne. Two birds, one stone.

When it was too cold to work in the garage I resorted to hand painting the Chrysler emblems. The two small round taillight reflectors did not prove satisfactory when done and were replaced with new ones found in the bicycle section of Pep Boys.

I delivered the car to Al's paint and body shop just before Christmas. Ginny, the girls and I spent New Year's in Las Vegas with the rest of my family who live there. We returned home January 6 and I got a call from Al that afternoon, telling me the car was done. I couldn't wait to see it. The weather that day was sort of on the gloomy side and I thought the lighting in Al's shop wouldn't be good enough to view the car properly, as it was getting darker by the minute. I grabbed my high-powered flashlight and headed to Palmdale.

When I got to Al's shop I couldn't believe my own eyes. The car looked great, but as I looked closer I could see little tiny specks of dust in the paint. Al could see my concern right off the bat and was somewhat offended that I had brought along a flashlight. I explained that I hadn't brought the flashlight purposely to inspect for dust particles but just to improve the light since the outside daylight was casting shadows.

In the long run bringing the flashlight got me a much better end result, because Al was so concerned about my satisfaction. A month later after the paint had a chance to cure, he spent another 2 days' labor free, color sanding and buffing the car out because of the dust specks. He was a man of his word, and when I reminded him of his promise that the car would look as good as anyone else could do for more money, he delivered.

The car sat idle in my garage until the middle of February just

Top: Hand painting the red detail of the hood chrome pieces required scuffing the chrome so that the paint would adhere. This was a tedious but fun job. *Bottom:* Nothing could be more relaxing than to sit and watch Saturday morning cartoons with the girls, drink coffee, paint the detail on my chrome parts and call around searching for parts. This is living, I tell you!

With the upholstery done and the color sanding complete, it was time to start putting on the chrome.

letting the paint harden. I would heat the garage on the weekends using a kerosene stove borrowed from Mike, just to help the process along. Finally it went to Al for the color sanding, and when I got it back again it looked fabulous—a museum quality paint job. I felt a bit embarrassed when I saw it now, realizing this paint and body work would have cost a good $3000 elsewhere. I then bought Al and his family lunch and promised to return when the chrome was put back on. "Al, my friend, you did a spectacular deed in holding to your promise," I told him. One more bare bones trip back to Lancaster and Goliath would soon sparkle with the finishing touches.

I let the car sit a few weeks more while I finished painting on the red background detail of the front and rear Chrysler emblems. I also did this on the hood and side pieces that say "Chrysler New Yorker" and the rear taillight fairing that says "Fluid Drive." I found

The car was placed in the garage where the final work would take place soon.

a taillight lens repair kit for newer cars that contained clear resin and red and amber dye. I experimented with the clear resin adding red dye, and then coated the rear stop light lens from the inside. It completely changed the faded pink lens to a rich red that looked brand new. On the rear taillight housings there is a reflector that was also faded pink with age. The colored resin wouldn't restore the luster to these pieces but I found a perfect match just the same size, in the bicycle section of Pep Boys.

To cure my starter problems from before, I had to replace the starter solenoid. I removed the starter around the middle of March. I took it to Jason's Auto Parts in Palmdale and he sent it to a shop in the San Fernando Valley. The unit came back rebuilt for $96, but the same solenoid was installed. I put it into the car, but the problem persisted.

117

It was now necessary to protect Goliath from the elements before the chrome could be put in place. It was also a very cozy place to store everything else.

Back at Jason's, Gary the owner gave me the address of the repair place. Gary phoned ahead and when I arrived they were expecting me. We bench tested the unit and it worked fine. I explained my problem of starting after the starter was installed. The guy there called around, but couldn't find a replacement solenoid. He said if I could find one he would pay for it and make things right by me. After all I had traveled a long distance to resolve the problem. I searched the ads in *Hemmings Motor News* and came up with one in Windsor Locks, Connecticut, for $48 plus shipping, for a total of $55. I received the solenoid in the mail, installed it onto the starter and presto—perfect starts every time. I took the bill to Jason's and he refunded me the $55. It sure makes it nice when people understand.

Also about the middle of March I began the installation of the chrome. The car began to take on a whole new appearance with each

The back of the car was ready to receive its new jewelry.

piece of chrome added. Finally after more than a year of hard work and fun, Goliath was starting to show signs of a true restoration. To me it was amazing and gratifying. Within just a few short months, the paint, upholstery and chrome had brought it all together. The new chrome taillight accented the new rubber pads that stuck out from underneath, protecting metal parts from touching. The new rubber molding on the trunk and the red background paint on the lettered pieces really jumped right out at you. The car looked as good as, if not better than, the day it rolled off the assembly line.

The final chrome strip along the upper left rear fender was popped into place on Sunday, March 29, 1992—Ginny's birthday, I kid you not.

9

Goliath's Second Life

I was ready for the debut. Ginny, Emily, Sarah and I all piled inside for our first ride (again). This time, though, it was different from ever before. This time it wasn't just a 1948 Chrysler traveling down the road, but a brand new shiny, sparkling, star-studded museum piece. When we rolled down the streets everyone looked, pointed, oohed, and aahed. I instructed the girls on an important point during that very first ride when I almost caught myself committing a serious error: You can't pick your nose at stop signs; everyone is watching!

The feeling you get driving a shiny old car is as if you are driving something that no one has ever seen before. You might as well be tooling around in the first Galactic Star Pacer for the interest it attracts. Seeing an old restored relic brings back many memories for many people, and stories abound.

When I honk the horn it broadcasts a tone that makes people smile and wave. The feeling of driving a car like this can only be explained as the most rewarding sense of pride and accomplishment that I have ever experienced. It is hard to express the joy and elation. If you have ever restored a car before, you know what I'm talking about, and if you plan to restore one in the future, you can look forward to the feeling.

In late April, after Goliath had stacked up a few hundred miles, the shifter began getting caught between two gears. I drove the car

Restorers know the job is never done, but here it is.

around seeking input and at Dave Miller's Transmission Specialties I found the right man to do the job. Dave's father had raised him in the business and was now retired, but, Dave knew what to do. He removed and disassembled the transmission to find a gear tooth chipped, and a slider pin broken. The total repair cost was $548.

Shortly after the transmission was overhauled retired NASA co-worker Clint Johnson, "Mr. Studebaker," introduced me to the Antelope Valley Region chapter of the Antique Automobile Club of America. Clint and I had never known each other per se, because by the time I started working out at Dryden, he was already retired. He contacted me though a mutual friend at NASA after reading the article written some time ago in the NASA newsletter. He asked Bill Clark if that guy restoring the car still worked out there. Bill gave him my phone number and he gave me a call inviting me to come on out and see his Studebakers—he had at least 10.

Step inside; shall we take the park route?

When I drove out to Clint's, he looked over Goliath and sponsored me into the club. That was back in 1992 and my family and I are still members. I have served on the local board of directors for six years. Three of those years I have served as club president. Goliath has run flawlessly year after year, accumulating over 25,000 miles since restoration.

Our club participates in 11 local parades around the Antelope Valley. We support many other community events such as the Lancaster Convalescent Hospital car display, the annual Poppy Festival, the Olde Towne Site Festival, and the Antelope Valley Fair and Alfalfa Festival. We participate in weddings, ice cream socials, football games and the grand openings of new roads. We have two annual events that are especially near and dear to us: a barbecue at the Groven Ranch and the annual car games.

The car games differ from year to year but my favorites are the

Ginny was beaming as broadly as I was as Goliath gleamed in the sun.

Potato Stabbing (Ginny and I took first place in 1999) and the balancing competition. We have a teeter totter that we drive up onto, one vehicle at a time, and the object is to balance your car. We also have a stop on a dime competition in which contestants drive a distance of 25 yards and must stop their right rear center axle closest to the dime. We have a Gentleman's Race in which you drive a distance to where your partner is sitting in a chair, shut off the vehicle, exit, cross to the other side, open the door for your partner, go back around, get in and drive off in the shortest amount of time. (This is really fun to watch when the person has to hand crank a Model T.) People in our club range from 12 years old (youth participation is encouraged) to 250 years old. That's right, we have one guy who's 249.

Top: Once a year in August, for the past 8 years, Goliath has pleased adults and children alike, as an entrant in the annual Antelope Valley Fair and Alfalfa Parade. *Bottom:* Goliath awaits the beginning of the Mojave Gold Rush event.

Poised for the Palmdale Christmas parade, Goliath is a sure winner.

Our local chapter is a collection of the greatest folks on earth. The diversity within the group is such that one might make the acquaintance of a housewife, an engineer, a mechanic, a rocket scientist, a salesman, a retired ol' fart, a manager, a painter, a plumber or any other person you can name. The Antelope Valley Region was officially chartered on February 4, 1960, and many of the founding members are still participating.

It was in June 1993, a little less than a year after I had joined the club, that I had the opportunity to show Gertrude Montrose the finished car. About ten of us club members had volunteered for a display of old vehicles for the Annual Old Town Site Festival. The sun was shining bright and we all had parked on the street with the cars all neatly in a row.

Mrs. Montrose approached while I was standing next to Goliath, talking to another spectator. "Remember me?" she said. I couldn't believe my eyes when I turned around. She stood there at the open driver's door, holding onto the doorpost. I'm not certain if she was addressing the car or me. "Mrs. Montrose!" I said, recognizing her at once. "How are you?" She didn't answer, but just slid into the driver's seat and grasped the huge steering wheel with both hands. "You have done a wonderful job," she said. "I raised my family in this car." A tear came to her eye and the tone of her voice changed. I said "Thank you" and told her that I had visited the house but found no one at home. she told me that she and Saul had separated and that she now lived in a townhouse by herself. Her daughter Melinda was with her and she too had approached the car by now. She nodded and smiled in approval of Goliath.

I noticed something at that moment that

Emily Rose Floyd poses for a photo by Dad at the park after the California City Tortoise Days Parade.

made sense of a point that had long puzzled me. As I looked at Mrs. Montrose holding the steering wheel I could see that the large diamond ring on her hand was the reason for several scratches on the driver's side wing window. It takes a push of the thumb and a rotation of the hand to open this window. Those marks had been made by the diamond as she rotated the handle.

Mrs. Montrose remained seated in the car for some time, just looking around, touching and commenting to Melinda. Soon the two of them strolled outside and around the car where Melinda stopped to explain to me how she used to stand up in the rear seat

The Gentleman's Race

Ginny's father, Don Neff (left foreground) witnesses his daughter's performance in the Gentleman's Race.

holding onto the blanket rope.* She entered the car on the passenger side and opened the glove box, touched the dashboard and felt the newly upholstered seats. Both appeared very happy as they wandered off after we exchanged good-byes and phone numbers.

It was much later, in fact soon after I had submitted this material for possible publication, that Saul Montrose and I

*Not often seen in newer cars, a blanket rope was usually a cord attached behind the drivers seat to drape a blanket for use when cold winter or night driving did not allow enough heat to stay warm.

Winners of the 1999 Potato Stabbing competition.

would meet again. I wanted Saul's permission to use his name in recounting Goliath's history, so I had to do a little detective work. Luckily my first avenue to contact Saul was fruitful. I opened the local phone book and looked for his name, and lo and behold, there it was. I dialed the number, he answered, and I announced myself. I explained my need for his permission and gave him a short account of the car; he agreed in two seconds. He wanted to see the car, and the drive to where he now lived was about a fifteen-minute jaunt. Saul was a very active person and it was not until my third choice of meeting times that his calendar was open for a visit.

Saul was waiting outside, resting on a park bench chatting with a friend as I rounded the uphill curve on his street. I watched him stand up, tap his friend on the should and point towards the car and me with the other hand. He was visibly excited, smiling from ear to ear. I stopped the car in front of the two men and both of them gave a thumbs-up sign, shaking their heads in approval. Parking was not allowed where I stopped, so Saul bade a good-bye to his friend and the two of us climbed inside and headed off for about a five-mile ride. When we returned to the parking area near Saul's apartment he insisted on showing me his 1976 Volare station wagon. A Chrysler man to the end, he exclaimed. The car was 23 years old and indeed a testament to Mr. Montrose's dedicated care. He asked if I wanted to see the maintenance book. He had kept a record book on this car as he had done with Goliath.

We had a high-energy visit and he

Emily Rose Floyd stands proudly next to her oil painting of Goliath, for which she received an honorable mention at the 1998 Antelope Valley Fair. I had no knowledge of this painting until I saw it on display. It now graces the wall behind my desk at work.

told me again of the many vacations and joyrides he and his family had taken in the car. He touched the car with smooth and delicate strokes as he reminisced of the past. We took photos from several angles and it was time to leave. Saul signed my release form so that I could use his name. His daughter Melinda came by for a brief visit as well and told me that Gertrude was now in Colorado staying with her brother. The good-byes were emotional for Saul and I promised to deliver a copy of this book when it came out.

As Saul could probably tell, no other time in my life has been as rewarding as these years that I have enjoyed Goliath's magic and an ever closer bond with my family. Recently I have been able to share that magic with another special person too.

In the spring of 1995, while working as a volunteer at the Lancaster Poppy Festival, Ginny met a woman who was sponsoring a community booth for Big Brothers of Greater Los Angeles. Knowing that our two girls had reached an age at which their interests had shifted toward dance, piano, gymnastics and sewing, and away from old cars, the garage and the things that Dad did, Ginny took note of the program and soon asked me if I would be interested in participating.

One thing led to another, and in the spring of 1996 I was matched up with Brandon Krick, a fine 10-year-old boy who had gone through some difficult experiences at a critical time in his life, much as I had when young. Brandon and I have been matched for

Luckily Brandon has a strong interest in cars, which gives us a special bond.

four years now and have enjoyed many activities together. Soon to be 15, he has an avid interest in old cars, and we are eager to begin a restoration project together. It gives me great satisfaction to have a friend like Brandon to share these experiences with.

On a visit to the Dryden Flight Research Center Brandon takes part in the launch of an SR-71. He assisted NASA test pilot Ed Schneider in suiting.

Afterword

My friend Fred Ducane never got to see the finished car. Shortly after Thanksgiving 1991 he went home to Fort Worth, Texas. Because we were both busy at the time we managed only a brief good-bye. I phoned him many times after he left and we always had hopes of his coming back out to California, or of my going to see him in Texas. But it would never happen.

A dreadful phone call came in January 1995. It was Mike Bondy, telling me the terrible news of Fred's death. He had suffered a massive coronary, according to the information Mike had received.

As I hung up the phone I felt flushed, overcome with emotion. It was hard to turn and tell Ginny the news without collapsing into tears. I spoke to her from across the room, repeating the awful facts, as she stood at the kitchen sink. Tears formed in my eyes as I faced the dining room window looking into the back yard, pain gripping my gut. Fighting a quiver in my lower lip, I took a deep breath, exhaled, and said to myself, "What a fine person Fred was." To me he had been a father, a brother, and most of all, a caring friend. The kind you love.

Mike and I later discussed attending Fred's funeral, but in the end we did not. Fred was a single divorced man and we did not know his children or other family. The ritual of seeing strangers cry over my friend in a casket seemed unnecessary to me, and Mike agreed.

My good friend and confidant pictured here in a fine pose, preparing to work on the carburetor.

For my part, I wanted to spend my time coping with his death by reflecting on the fond memories that I still treasure. We had shared more good times than most people know in a lifetime.

I think often of the time Fred and I spent together, working or just talking, sometimes discussing our philosophies of life. When Fred and I were in the garage working on various stages of Goliath's restoration or just relaxing with a cold one, he always had a story to tell. My favorite was a tale he told me about the early development of cruise control.

Fred had worked for Chrysler Corporation at the test track in the early 1960s, and his job had often entailed going around and around the track for hours testing tires, electrical components or engine endurance after a modification. One particular day he and one of the factory engineers were doing an electrical test, and Fred was driving while the engineer monitored the instruments connected

Fred was very proud of his contributions in the restoration of Goliath. Here he has just finished painting the intake and exhaust manifolds.

to the unit. A friend was also on the track testing in an Imperial, circling the track at about twice the speed Fred and the engineer were going.

Then on one lap Fred and the engineer noticed there was no one in the Imperial's driver's seat, but his friend was in the back seat laughing and waving as he went by. This continued for quite some time. At the end of the day Fred went over to his friend and found out that he was testing a new device called cruise control. What he had done that was so clever was to tie two ropes to the steering wheel and route them under the seat to the rear. After he got going and started his test time, he set the cruise control, hopped over into the back seat and continued driving using only the ropes to steer the car. There was no need to stop, but if he had to disengage the cruise control he merely reached over the seat. Fred would laugh so hard telling this story that you would think he was about to cry.

That's how I like to remember Fred. He will forever be in my thoughts.

Appendix: Restoration Expense Ledger

2/4/91   Purchase $650.00

2/9/91   Towing $30.00

2/23/91   Degreaser $5.50
          Buy N Save Auto Parts
          Lancaster, CA

2/23/91   Gunk and paint $5.61
          Pep Boys
          Lancaster, CA

2/23/91   Axle seals and oil $48.05
          Jason's Auto Parts
          Palmdale, CA

2/23/91   3rd member $59.00
          Glendale Auto Salvage
          Lancaster, CA

3/23/91   Labor (install pinion seal) $15.00
          Yarman Drive Shafts
          Lancaster, CA

3/23/91	Jack stands $10.68
	Chief Auto Parts
	Lancaster, CA

3/24/91	Torque wrench $8.51
	Chief Auto Parts
	Lancaster, CA

4/2/91	Rear wheel cylinders, P/N W010488 . . . . $64.00
	(Safe Line MFG.)
	Kaos Auto Parts
	Lancaster, CA

4/9/91	Front wheel cylinders, P/N 10580/81/82/83 . . . . $68.00
	(Safe Line MFG.)
	Kaos Auto Parts
	Lancaster, CA

4/12/91	Brake flex hoses, P/N Fc10304 (Front L/R), ... $30.60
	P/N Fc10595 (Rear)
	Kaos Auto Parts
	Lancaster, CA

4/12/91	Brake master cylinder, P/N 41-53 NOS $75.00
	Old Cars Parts
	Indianapolis, IN

4/13/91	Degreaser/pan $10.67
	Buy N Save Auto Parts
	Lancaster, CA

4/25/91	Reline front brake shoes $38.00
	North Division Brake
	Lancaster, CA

5/4/91	Brake bleed fitting $1.17
	Buy N Save Auto Parts
	Lancaster, CA

5/8/91   Reprinted shop manual, Chrysler 1941–48 .... $29.00
Draglich Discount Auto Lit.
Minneapolis, MN

5/10/91   Brake return springs $22.00
Jason's Auto Parts
Palmdale, CA

5/18/91   Universal joint $50.00
Yarman Drive Shafts
Lancaster, CA

5/21/91   Grease $10.75
Pep Boys
Lancaster, CA

5/26/91   Battery, P/N 011345 .... $28.88
Pep Boys
Lancaster, CA

6/5/91   Carb overhaul kit, P/N Ye-405 .... $31.00
Pro Antique Auto Parts
Windsor Locks, CT

6/5/91   Spare tire (used) $24.61
Apollo Tire
Lancaster, CA

6/5/91   Hood release cable $16.04
North Division Brake
Lancaster, CA

6/6/91   Registration, tax, transfer, penalties $75.00
California DMV
Lancaster, CA

6/15/91   Spark plugs, cap, condenser $42.00
Pro Antique Auto Parts
Indianapolis, IN

6/22/91   Meat thermometer $3.85
                  Thrifty Drug Store
                  Lancaster, CA

7/2/91   WD-40, silicone spray, paint $16.52
                  Monte's Auto Parts
                  Lancaster, CA

7/16/91   Engine overhaul gaskets, Chrysler 8 cyl. 1948 . . . . . $75.00
                  Terril Machine Co.
                  DeLeon, TX

7/16/91   Radiator wrought & flushed $25.00
                  ABC Radiator
                  Lancaster, CA

7/16/91   Water pump overhaul kit $45.00
                  Mitchells Motor Parts
                  Columbus, OH

7/17/91   Brass battery terminals (original equipment) $9.74
                  Auto Parts Unlimited
                  Lancaster, CA

7/17/91   Misc. engine flex hoses $29.05
                  Pep Boys
                  Lancaster, CA

7/17/91   Freeze plugs, thermostat, gaskets, starter boot, ... $58.08
                    hose, belt
                  Jason's Auto Parts
                  Palmdale, CA

7/18/91   High temp. engine paint $8.56
                  R&E Racing
                  Lancaster, CA

7/18/91   Mineral spirits $9.71
                  Standard Brands Paint
                  Lancaster, CA

7/21/91	Shock absorbers, P/N 2c6 F25 (2 EA.), ... $87.00
	P/N 1135542 (2 EA.)
	Kanter Auto Products
	Boonton, NJ

8/2/91   Gunk/paint $25.51
              Pep Boys
              Lancaster, CA

8/9/91   Vacuum advance, decals, rubber seal for radiator $49.50
              Mitchell's Motor Parts
              Columbus, OH

8/12/91   Water temperature gauge $27.77
              Pep Boys
              Lancaster, CA

8/12/91   Oil/bolts $17.83
              Chief Auto Parts
              Lancaster, CA

8/13/91   Paint $9.61
              Pep Boys
              Lancaster, CA

8/16/91   Allthread, paint, nuts $5.31
              Buy N Save Auto Parts
              Lancaster, CA

8/17/91   Ignition rotor, 1 spark plug $3.52
              Kaos Auto Parts
              Lancaster, CA

8/18/91   Ignition wires, tap $41.57
              Don's Auto Parts
              Lancaster, CA

8/23/91   Tires $229.27
              Apollo Tire
              Lancaster, CA

8/25/91   Gasket paper $3.85
Buy N Save Auto Parts
Lancaster, CA

8/30/91   Rebuilt water pump (spare) $65.00
Kaos Auto Parts
Lancaster, CA

9/2/91   Spray undercoat, paint $16.74
Buy N Save Auto Parts
Lancaster, CA

9/8/91   Antifreeze, fuel additive $20.84
Buy N Save Auto Parts
Lancaster, CA

9/12/91   Rebuild generator, voltage reg. $96.00
Auto Parts Unlimited
Lancaster, CA

9/20/91   Oil, freeze plugs $27.66
Pep Boys
Lancaster, CA

9/21/91   Battery hold-down bracket $5.28
Buy N Save Auto Parts
Lancaster, CA

9/25/91   Rebuilt fuel pump (spare) $61.00
Kanter Auto Parts
Boonton, NJ

10/5/91   Upholstery deposit $800.00
Bob Vasquez
Lancaster, CA

10/8/91   Door sill grommets, misc. rubber $43.12
Steele Rubber Co.
Denver, NC

10/22/91   Bulk rubber strip for trunk, rubber pads $47.20
         for tail/brake light
         Mitchell Motor Parts
         Columbus, OH

10/26/91   Paint and body repair $1500.00
         Adonai (Al Simperson)
         Palmdale, CA

10/29/91   Chrome deposit $250.00
         Décor Plating
         Hawthorne, CA

10/??/91   Window channel (whiskers) $275.00
         Healy Auto Glass
         Lancaster, CA

12/6/91   Upholstery, balance $800.00
         Bob Vasquez
         Lancaster, CA

12/16/91   Chrome, balance $750.00
         Décor Plating
         Lancaster, CA

2/24/92   Car duster $16.00

3/??/92   Rebuild starter, solenoid $96.00
         Jason's Auto Parts
         Palmdale, CA

4/25/92   Transmission overhaul $548.00
         Transmission Specialties
         Lancaster, CA

Index